BRIGHT NOTES

ANTONY AND CLEOPATRA BY WILLIAM SHAKESPEARE

Intelligent Education

INFLUENCE PUBLISHERS

Nashville, Tennessee

BRIGHT NOTES: Antony and Cleopatra
www.BrightNotes.com

No part of this publication may be used or reproduced in any manner whatsoever without written permission, except in the case of brief quotations in critical articles and reviews. For permissions, contact Influence Publishers http://www.influencepublishers.com

ISBN: 978-1-645425-50-2 (Paperback)
ISBN: 978-1-645425-51-9 (eBook)

Published in accordance with the U.S. Copyright Office Orphan Works and Mass Digitization report of the register of copyrights, June 2015.

Originally published by Monarch Press.
William Walsh, 1964
2020 Edition published by Influence Publishers.

Interior design by Lapiz Digital Services. Cover Design by Thinkpen Designs.

Printed in the United States of America.

Library of Congress Cataloging-in-Publication Data forthcoming.
Names: Intelligent Education
Title: BRIGHT NOTES: Antony and Cleopatra
Subject: STU004000 STUDY AIDS / Book Notes

CONTENTS

1) Introduction to William Shakespeare — 1

2) Introduction to Antony and Cleopatra — 6

3) Textual Analysis — 12
   - Act 1 — 12
   - Act 2, Scenes 1-4 — 33
   - Act 2, Scenes 5-7 — 48
   - Act 3, Scenes 1-6 — 67
   - Act 3, Scenes 7-13 — 83
   - Act 4 — 99
   - Act 5 — 122

4) Character Analyses — 140

5) Critical Commentary — 150

6) Essay Questions and Answers — 166

7) Subject Bibliography and Guide to Research Papers — 171

8) General Biography and Criticism — 176

INTRODUCTION TO WILLIAM SHAKESPEARE

On April 26, 1564, William Shakespeare, son of John Shakespeare and Mary Arden, was christened in Holy Trinity Church, Stratford-on-Avon. His birthday is traditionally placed three days before. He was the eldest of four boys and two girls born to his father, a well-to-do glover and trader, who also held some minor offices in the town government. He probably attended the local free school, where he picked up the "small Latin and less Greek" that Ben Jonson credits him with. ("Small" Latin to that knowledgeable classicist meant considerably more than it does today.) As far as is known, this was the extent of Shakespeare's formal education. In November of 1582, when he was eighteen, a license was issued for his marriage to Ann Hathaway, a Stratford neighbor eight years older than himself. The following May their child Susanna was christened in the same church as her father. While it may be inferred from this that his marriage was a forced one, such an inference is not necessary; engagement at that time was a legally binding contract and was sometimes construed as allowing conjugal rights. Their union produced two more children, twins Judith and Hamnet, christened in February, 1585. Shortly thereafter Shakespeare left Stratford for a career in London. What he did during these years - until we pick him up, an established playwright, in 1592 - we do not know, as no records exist. It is presumed that he served an apprenticeship in the theatre, perhaps as a provincial trouper, and eventually won himself a place as an actor. By 1594 he was a successful dramatist with the Lord Chamberlain's company (acting groups had noble protection and patronage), having produced the *Comedy of Errors* and the *Henry VI* trilogy, probably in collaboration with older, better established dramatists. When the plague closed the London theatres for many months of 1593-94, he found himself without a livelihood. He promptly turned his hand to poetry (although written in verse, plays were not considered as dignified as poetry), writing two long narrative poems, *Venus and Adonis* and *The Rape of Lucrece*. He dedicated them to the Earl of Southampton, undoubtedly receiving some recompense. The early nineties also saw the first of Shakespeare's **sonnets** circulating in manuscript, and later finding their way into print. In his early plays - mostly chronicle histories glorifying England's past, and light comedies - Shakespeare sought for popular success and achieved it. In 1599 he was able to buy a share in the Globe Theatre, where he acted and where his plays were performed. His ever-increasing financial success enabled him to buy a good deal of real estate in his native Stratford, and by 1605 he was able to retire from acting. Shortly thereafter he began to spend most of his time in Stratford, to which he retired around 1610. Very little is known of his life after he left London. He died on April 23, 1616, in Stratford, and was buried there. In 1623 the First Folio edition of his complete works was published by a group of his friends as a testimonial to his memory. This was a very rare tribute, because at the time plays were generally considered to be inferior literature, not really worthy of publication. These scanty facts, together with some information about the dates of his plays, are all that is definitely known about the greatest writer in the history of English literature. The age in which Shakespeare lived was not as concerned with keeping accurate records as we are, and any further details about Shakespeare's life have been derived from educated guesses based on knowledge of his time. Shakespeare's plays fall into three major groups according to the periods in his development when he wrote them:

EARLY COMEDIES AND HISTORIES

The first group consists of romantic comedies such as *A Midsummer Night's Dream* (1593-5), and of strongly patriotic histories such as *Henry V* (1599). The early comedies are full of farce and slapstick, as well as exuberant poetry. Their plots are complicated and generally revolve around a young love relationship. The histories are typical of the robust, adventurous English patriotism of the Elizabethan era, when England had achieved a position of world dominance and power.

THE GREAT TRAGEDIES

The second period, beginning with *Hamlet* and ending with *Antony and Cleopatra*, is the period of the great tragedies: *Hamlet* (1602); *Othello* (1604); *King Lear* (1605); *Macbeth* (1606); and *Antony and Cleopatra* (1607-8). Shakespeare seems to have gone through a mental crisis at this time. His vision of the world darkens, and he sees life as an **epic** battle between the forces of good and evil, between order and chaos within man and in the whole universe. The forces for good win out in the end over evil, which is self-defeating. But the victory of the good is at great cost and often comes at the point of death. It is a moral victory, not a material one. These tragedies center on a great man who, because of some flaw in his makeup, or some error he commits, brings death and destruction down upon himself and those around him. They are generally considered the greatest of Shakespeare's plays.

THE LATE ROMANCES

In the third period Shakespeare returns to romantic comedy. But such plays as *Cymbeline* (1609-10), *The Winter's Tale* (1610-11), and *The Tempest* (1611) are very different in point of view and structure from such earlier comedies as *Much Ado About Nothing* (1599) and *Twelfth Night* (1600). Each of these late romances has a situation potentially tragic, and there is much bitterness in them. Thus the destructive force of insane jealousy serves as the **theme** both of the tragedy, *Othello*, and the comedy, *The Winter's Tale*. They are serious comedies, replacing farce and slapstick with rich symbolism and supernatural events. They deal with such **themes** as sin and redemption, death and rebirth, and the conflict between nature and society, rather than with simple romantic love. In a sense they are deeply religious, although unconnected with any church dogma. In his last play, *The Tempest*, Shakespeare achieved a more or less serene outlook upon the world after the storm and stress of his great tragedies and the so-called "dark comedies."

SHAKESPEARE'S THEATRE

Shakespeare's plays were written for a stage very different from our own. Women, for instance, were not allowed to act; so female parts, even that of Cleopatra, were played by boy actors whose voices had not yet changed. The plays were performed on a long platform surrounded by a circular, unroofed theatre, and were dependent on natural daylight for lighting. There was no curtain separating the stage from the audience, nor were there act divisions. These were added to the plays by later editors. Because the stage jutted right into the audience, Shakespeare was able to achieve a greater intimacy with his spectators than modern playwrights can. The audience in the pit, immediately surrounding the stage, had to stand crowded together throughout the play. Its members tended to be lower class Londoners who would frequently comment aloud on the action of the play and break into fights. Anyone who attended the plays in the pit did so at the risk of having his pockets picked, of catching a disease, or, at best, of being jostled about by the crude "groundlings." The aristocratic and merchant classes, who watched the plays from seats in the galleries, were spared most of the physical discomforts of the pit.

ITS ADVANTAGES

There were certain advantages, however, to such a theatre. Because complicated scenic, lighting and sound effects were impossible, the playwright had to rely on the power of his words to create scenes in the audience's imagination. The rapid changes of scene and vast distances involved in *Antony and Cleopatra*, for instance, although they create a problem for modern producers, did not for Shakespeare. Shakespeare did not rely - as the modern realistic theatre does - on elaborate stage scenery to create atmosphere and locale. For these, as for battle scenes involving large numbers of people, Shakespeare relied on the suggestive power of his poetry to quicken the imagination of his audience. Elizabethan audiences were very lively anyway, and quick to catch any kind of word play. Puns, jokes, and subtle poetic effects made a greater impression on them than on modern audiences, who are less alert to language.

ANTONY AND CLEOPATRA

INTRODUCTION

This play is more celebrated for its poetry than its drama. It is very loosely constructed, especially the middle part - Acts 2, 3, 4 - with too many fragmentary scenes trying to cover too vast a panorama over too long a period of time. It is chronicle, not true drama. What dramatic tautness it possesses comes from its central conflict between Antony's love and his sense of duty, the siren call of Egypt and the pressing demands of Rome. But its real unity is established by the poetry. In *Antony and Cleopatra* Shakespeare's poetry achieves its greatest breadth and naturalness; he can turn everything, every experience, from the most exalted sentiment to the lowest command, into verse and even into poetry. Besides breadth of experience, there is depth of emotion. By means of the rhythm, images, figures, even sounds of the verse, he makes every experience not only talked about, but actually felt. In this play Shakespeare reaches a culmination and a turning point in his poetic development. And with it he passes from the great tragedies to the late romances.

ITS SOURCES

As usual with him, Shakespeare "stole" his story or plot; he is seldom original in this respect. He is original in how he combines his sources and reworks them in his plays. The main, predominant source for *Antony and Cleopatra* was Thomas North's 1579 translation into English of a French version by James Amyot of Plutarch's Lives of the Noble Grecians and Romanes, Compared. From Plutarch's biography of Marcus Antonius he took his story, setting, and most of his characters. He also adopted word for word, or very nearly, many of North's descriptions. The major characters, however, he changed somewhat, for brevity and greater drama. He played down Antony's worst traits as North describes them, although he did not whitewash his character entirely. Certainly Antony's attractive qualities are more conspicuous in Shakespeare than in North. To Cleopatra he did the opposite, made her coarser, more perverse and irritating than in North, and shifted his focus from the sexual to the psychological qualities of the notorious queen. This change may have been prompted by the use of a boy actor to play the part. Other plays on the same subject which may have influenced Shakespeare in writing his own were Samuel Daniels' *Cleopatra* (1594) and the Countess of Pembroke's *The Tragedie of Antonie*.

BRIEF SUMMARY OF ANTONY AND CLEOPATRA

The story of Antony's tragic love for Cleopatra begins long before the play. It is set against the background of great political upheaval in a turbulent period of Roman history. The love affair shares the grandeur of these events, and they are often referred to in its dramatization.

Julius Caesar, Gnaeus Pompeius (called The Great), and Marcus Crassus formed the first Roman Triumvirate or "three-man-rule" in 60 B. C. Seven years later (53 B. C.) Crassus was treacherously murdered by Orodes, King of Parthia, during a council of truce after his defeat on the plains of Mesopotamia. Caesar fell out with his remaining partner and defeated him in the battle of Pharsalia in northeast Greece in 48 B. C. Pompey fled and was subsequently killed on the Egyptian coast of Africa. That left Caesar the sole ruler. Jealous of Roman freedom and fearing Caesar's growing power, Marcus Brutus lent his efforts and prestige to Gaius Cassius's cabal to assassinate Caesar in 44 B. C. The story of their successful overthrow of Caesar and their subsequent defeat at Philippi in northeast Greece is dramatized in Shakespeare's *Julius Caesar*. Caesar's avengers were his closest friend and protégé, Marcus Antonius; his adopted heir, Octavius; and another friend, Lepidus. These three formed the second Triumvirate in 43 B. C. For purposes of administration they divided the Roman Empire into three parts. Octavius Caesar took under his aegis Italy and the western and northern provinces; Lepidus ruled over Africa - except for Egypt, which with all the conquered territories east of the Adriatic, was governed by Mark Antony. Marshaling his forces for a war against the Parthians to the east, Antony summoned Cleopatra to the city of Tarsus in Cilicia to answer accusations that she had aided Brutus and Cassius in their war against the Triumvirate. At their meeting he became so infatuated with her that he abandoned all his state affairs, his wife Fulvia's war against Caesar in Italy, and his own preparations against the Parthians, to follow Cleopatra back to Alexandria. And that is where our play finds him, caught up in the frivolous pleasures and pastimes of the Egyptian Court.

His action has given offense to both Fulvia and Caesar: to Fulvia because of his open betrayal of their marriage bond; to Caesar because Antony fails to assist him when he is threatened by Fulvia's war and by the conspiracy of Sextus Pompey. Sextus Pompey is the son of Gnaeus Pompey, one of the first Triumvirs, ultimately deposed by his partner Julius Caesar. Now the son inherits his great father's resentment against Caesar and his heirs, and claims his right to the imperial rule. He has formed a conspiracy with the help of some notorious pirates who operate off the Italian coast. From their base in Sicily they have raided the maritime provinces and eliminated coastal shipping. Meanwhile Caesar, never very popular, has been losing the allegiance of the people, who have gone over to Pompey and flocked to the seacoasts expecting an invasion.

News of Caesar's political crisis, of Fulvia's death and of a Parthian invasion shock Antony out of his lethargy. He becomes for a while the able statesman and general again, returning to Rome to patch up his differences with Caesar by marrying his widowed sister Octavia; frightening (by his very presence in Italy) Pompey into a treaty of peace; dispatching his Lieutenant Ventidius to check the Parthian invasion. But even in the midst of this activity, he knows it will be short lived. Acting on the advice of an Egyptian fortune teller, he resolves to return to Cleopatra in Alexandria. In the meantime, Ventidius trounces the Parthian invaders, as Antony and his bride set out for Athens. In her Egyptian court in Alexandria, Cleopatra has kept herself posted of Antony's affairs. When first she hears the report of his marriage, she flies into a rage, threatening to kill or maim the messenger who brings the news, beating him and frightening him away. When she is calmer, she pumps him for information about Octavia's appearance and behavior, and he, to save his skin, tells her the lies she wishes to hear. She resolves to win Antony back. In Athens Antony also hears disturbing news from Italy: that his brother-in-law has waged new wars against Pompey, made his will and read it publicly, and openly shown hostility toward his partner. Octavia insists on returning to Rome to patch up their differences before the breach widens beyond repair, while Antony readies his fleet to attack Caesar. Her mission is unsuccessful. Only two motives would be great enough to force Octavius into a war against Antony: (1) to protect his sister against insult or injury; (2) to protect himself against surprise attack. Antony's return to Cleopatra in Egypt and his war-preparations against Rome give Caesar both, and he moves quickly to gain the advantage of surprise. He transports his entire army to the southwest coast of Italy and sails across the Ionian Sea to capture Toryne before Antony has time to finish his preparations. Chief among these preparations is Cleopatra's insistence upon a sea battle and upon personally commanding her Egyptian navy in it. This proves disastrous when, in the midst of the battle, she turns and runs with all her ships - and Antony follows her. The defeat at Actium causes dissension in Antony's ranks, and several generals and much of his army desert him. Antony asks Caesar for terms of truce, but Caesar refuses and sends his ambassador Thidias to seduce Cleopatra to his side. Antony discovers them in time to prevent it. But Enobarbus, Antony's closest friend and subordinate, seeing Antony's frantic insecurity, and realizing his lord's judgment is warped, decides to desert to Caesar's side while Antony determines to fight to the death. The next day's battle Antony wins, and this makes him overconfident. But not for long. For on the second day he cockily decides to engage Caesar at sea again. This time his entire navy deserts him and surrenders to Caesar without a fight. Antony is broken by it; he accuses Cleopatra of betrayal and threatens to kill her. Out of fear, she locks herself in her mausoleum and sends him word she is dead. Hearing this news he tries to commit suicide but succeeds only in wounding himself mortally. As he lies dying another messenger from Cleopatra reveals the truth and he orders his soldiers to carry him to his mistress, where he dies in her arms. Left alone now, Cleopatra decides she cannot live without Antony and refuses to be taken a prisoner to Rome by Caesar. She decides to kill herself by the bite of a venomous serpent, an asp. Caesar uses every means to prevent her, but she outwits him finally and dies with her maids. He discovers her body and orders a state funeral to bury the dead lovers together.

ANTONY AND CLEOPATRA

TEXTUAL ANALYSIS

ACT 1

ACT 1, SCENE 1

The play opens upon the following political situation: Rome has extended its empire over most of the known world, from the British Isles to Parthia and Mesopotamia in the east, and from the African shore of the Mediterranean to Germany in the north. Much of its eastern empire has been conquered by Mark Antony who, together with Octavius Caesar and Lepidus, makes up the Triumvirate or ruling body of the empire. Octavius Caesar rules over Rome and the northern provinces, Lepidus over Africa, and Mark Antony over the east. Supposedly to govern his conquered territories, Antony has set up headquarters and remained in Egypt. Actually he has fallen in love with Cleopatra, queen of Egypt, which is one of his conquered kingdoms. Their love is the story of the play. It begins in Cleopatra's palace in Alexandria, the Egyptian capital. Two of Antony's lieutenants, Demetrius and Philo, are complaining in one of the rooms of the palace.

Comment

Since the theatres in Shakespeare's day did not use elaborate scenery but a rather bare stage for their productions, the descriptions of locale or scene are usually very general. While this meant that the author had to depend a great deal on the audience's imagination, it also enabled him to change scenes rapidly with a mere stroke of the pen. We shall see throughout the play how Shakespeare takes advantage of this freedom.

Philo condemns Antony's infatuation with Cleopatra outright. Their general, he tells Demetrius, has lost his manliness and given over his pursuit of war and conquest to pursue his lust instead. He "is become the bellows and the fan/ To cool a gipsy's lust."

Comment

This opening speech sets up the central conflict of the play. But it presents only one side or view of the question that will be resolved. The whole play revolves around the question of whether or not Antony is justified in loving Cleopatra and abandoning all else for her. Philo here presents the Roman point of view, that he is not. According to him, Antony merely dotes on Cleopatra. He conceives of her as "tawny" or dark in color, and so not a fit match for Antony, especially since she is a "gipsy," a person of little worth. And this "dotage" has caused Antony to neglect his duties to Rome and to become weak and effeminate in allowing himself to be dominated by the wily and capricious Cleopatra, especially since he has previously been famous for his bravery and military prowess. The Roman "ethic," that is, the code of conduct favored by Rome, is a martial one, emphasizing the virtues of manliness, discipline, and self-reliance.

Almost as if to give proof of Philo's speech, Antony, Cleopatra, and her servants enter, in a procession marked by oriental luxury and splendor. Philo, in an aside, promises Demetrius he shall see Antony, "the triple pillar of the world" (i.e., one of the three rulers of the world), become the plaything of a whore. And, indeed, Antony at once begins to exchange extravagant vows of love with Cleopatra. "There's beggary in the love that can be reckoned," cries Antony, expressing not only his love for Cleopatra but his contempt for the sound commercial account-keeping that has made Rome a great power. He is obviously annoyed when an attendant interrupts to announce a messenger from Rome. Antony refuses to see him. The business "grates" him, he says, and he demands "the sum" of it, quickly, so that he can turn back to Cleopatra. She, however, now begins to taunt him for being under the thumbs of Fulvia, his wife, and the boyish Caesar. (Octavius Caesar is in his early twenties. His youth, as compared to the other Triumvirs, is alluded to throughout. Despite his age, he is the leader of the Triumvirate.) Antony's reply is a ringing speech in which he renounces Rome's claims upon him, and determines to stay in Egypt with Cleopatra.

Comment

The Egyptian view is emerging, a direct contrast to the Roman one. The Egyptians love extravagant display, luxury, and pleasure, which the Romans scorn; and they in turn scorn the coldness, prudence, and calculating self-interest of Rome. Antony is a man in the middle, accused by Philo of being Cleopatra's fool, and by Cleopatra of being Fulvia's and Caesar's. He does indeed love Cleopatra; whether, as Philo complains, this love has made him womanish and a traitor to himself, remains to be seen. "The nobleness of life is to do thus," Antony exclaims, and the conflict of ideas is clear: Is it nobler to love passionately and magnificently, sacrificing in the process the worldly greatness which would otherwise be his due; or, by the exercise of reason and self-control, to sacrifice that love on the altar of fame and military glory? Antony, at this point, is of a mind to follow the former course: "Let Rome in Tiber melt ... We stand up peerless." In other words, for all he cares, Rome may be washed away for a love like theirs justifies itself, and they cannot be blamed for renouncing everything for it.

Cleopatra, however, ignores Antony's grand rhetoric and continues to tease him. She wonders why Antony married Fulvia, since he does not love her, and whether, perhaps, the same fate will someday be hers. She urges him to see the messengers, although of course it is to her interest for Antony not to be in contact with Rome. Antony, who feels that he merits her praise for refusing to see them, talks only of love and pleasure; when Cleopatra interrupts with "Hear the ambassadors," he chides her for being so difficult: "Fie, wrangling queen." He is determined to fill every minute of their lives with pleasure, "for the love of Love"; there is no time to waste. They exit without hearing Caesar's messenger, and Demetrius, realizing that this is a grave insult, tells Philo that he is convinced that the rumors which have reached Rome of Antony's debasement are true.

SUMMARY

The opening scene has set the general mood of the play in the following ways:

1. It has introduced the lovers, Antony and Cleopatra.

2. It has given us a glimpse of their love and of the conflict surrounding it.

3. It has shown us the "Roman view" of this love, which condemns it, and the "Egyptian view," which praises it.

4. It has presented Antony's dilemma: Whether to choose Rome and Caesar's friendship or to reject both for Cleopatra and her Egyptian way of life.

ACT 1, SCENE 2

In another room of the palace an Egyptian soothsayer (a kind of fortune teller) is revealing what life holds in store for Cleopatra's various attendants: Alexas, her male servant; Mardian, her eunuch; Charmian and Iras, her maids. Silently looking on and listening to the revelry and lewd joking are a group of Roman soldiers: Enobarbus, Antony's trusted lieutenant and close friend; Lamprius, Rannius, and Lucillius. Occasionally Enobarbus adds his rude voice to the coarse exchange. But for the most part their silence represents a sober Roman reprimand to the loose conversation.

Comment

Some critics have taken Lamprius to be the soothsayer. But this does not seem probable because the name is too Roman-sounding for the obviously Egyptian character, and because this same soothsayer appears later with Antony in Rome and there is not called Lamprius (Act 2, Scene 3).

Alexas seems to have been teasing Charmian by predicting for her a husband whom she will cuckold. Charmian hopes he is right: "O that I knew this husband, which, you say, must charge his horns with garlands!" (A cuckold is a man whose wife has committed adultery. As a sign of her infidelity he is jokingly said to grow horns.) She asks the soothsayer to confirm the good fortune Alexas has promised. He replies that he cannot change her fate, only foresee it. She hopes for several husbands and many children; what he tells her, however, is that she will outlive Cleopatra, and that the part of her life which is to come will be less pleasant than that which she has already lived.

Comment

The atmosphere of the scene is curiously mixed or contradictory, like a summer sun-shower. Although the general tone is light and comic, the pronouncements of the soothsayer foreshadow the tragic events to come. His predictions deal with the deaths of Cleopatra and Charmian in language full of dramatic **irony**. The statement that Charmian will outlive Cleopatra sounds innocent enough at this point; it is only after we have witnessed the play in its entirety that we realize how sinister it is. Charmian will indeed outlive her mistress, but only by a minute or two. And she will not have the long life she loves better than figs. But the asp by whose bite she dies will be hidden in a basket of figs. It is not clear whether the soothsayer knows exactly what the outcome will be, but his statement that he is powerless to avert it, whatever it is, is significant.

Much sexual joking follows. The women wish for many children; because of the pleasure of begetting them, the soothsayer implies. Enobarbus knows what their fortunes will be at least that night: "drunk to bed." Iras, turning to palmistry, claims that hers is a palm which shows that she is nothing if not chaste; Charmian retorts ironically that if she is chaste, then the overflowing of the Nile is a portent of famine, when in fact it is just the opposite. The soothsayer claims simply that the fortunes of Iras and Charmian are alike, and refuses to give particulars. Charmian begs for news of a husband who is sexually well-endowed, and, in mock-spite, wishes for Alexas a wife who is not, followed by one who will cuckold him. She begs the goddess Isis to grant her this wish, even if she denies her something more important later on.

Comment

Isis was an Egyptian goddess, patroness of fertility and of the sexual act which causes it. "A woman that cannot go" is a frigid woman who cannot perform the sexual act. This casual mention becomes very important to the **imagery** later on when Cleopatra dresses herself as an incarnation of Isis (Act 4, Scene 7). Isis was also associated with the changing moon, and this ties in with the moon **imagery** and the notion of fickleness, the waxing and waning of fortune, behind it. This scene is also rich in **allusion** and **irony**. The Egyptian court is seen as gay and fun-loving, in contrast to the unsmiling seriousness of the Roman soldiers uncomfortably watching it. The constant references to fertility and fruitfulness serve to identify the Egyptians with these qualities, which, like the sexual nature of man in this play, are both life-giving and destructive. It is significant that Enobarbus, who is a Roman, takes part in all this: he is not the prude that Philo is, but his good-humored cynicism about the validity of the soothsayer's prognostications will prove to be a mistake.

Enobarbus says, "Hush, here comes Antony," but it is Cleopatra who enters.

Comment

Enobarbus obviously does not want Antony to hear the jokes about cuckoldry, since he is being unfaithful to Fulvia with Cleopatra. The fact that it is Cleopatra who enters instead is explained later by the queen herself. The purpose of the surprise is to show us how swiftly changing is Antony's mood. One moment he is all gaiety, walking with his mistress; the next, he goes morosely off by himself.

Cleopatra asks for Antony; when last seen, she says. "He was disposed to mirth; but on the sudden/ A Roman thought hath struck him" (that is, either a thought of Rome, which sobered him, or a thought such as a Roman might have, implying that Romans are sour and incapable of mirth). Antony enters with a messenger from Rome, possibly the one he would not hear before. The messenger is afraid to tell Antony some bad news, and Antony magnanimously assures him that he, the messenger, will not be blamed for it.

Comment

This is in marked contrast to Cleopatra's treatment of the messenger who brings her news of Antony's marriage (Act 2, Scene 5), and shows the cooler judgment and sense of justice of the Roman.

Actually the messenger brings a military dispatch from the eastern frontier where Labienus and his Parthian armies have invaded Antony's territory. Antony thinks he is withholding his real message out of deference and fear. He thinks it is that his reputation in Rome is suffering, and that Fulvia is angry.

Before he can learn the truth, another messenger enters with news from Sicyon; Antony, caught up in this whirl of portentous activity and excited by all the comings and goings, muses: "These strong Egyptian fetters I must break/ Or lose myself in dotage." A third messenger enters and announces, without preamble, that Fulvia, Antony's wife, is dead.

Comment

It is to be noted that Antony, although he previously disavowed Rome and his responsibilities in favor of love, has now reversed his position completely. He now agrees, in effect, with Philo, that he is a prisoner of Cleopatra's charms, and he even uses the same word which Philo employed, "dotage," to characterize himself. It is in this excited and self-critical mood that he receives the news that Fulvia is dead from messengers whom he is now vitally interested in hearing.

Antony takes the news stoically and chides himself for desiring Fulvia's death, as he obviously did, because it would leave him free to marry or live with Cleopatra. The effect of the news is to strengthen his resolve to break off from Cleopatra, and resume his rightful place as leader of the world; his idleness, he thinks, is responsible for this and many other ills. All business, he summons Enobarbus and bids him make ready to leave without telling him why; Enobarbus retorts in a jocular tone, and makes what, under the circumstances, is an unfortunate joke about Cleopatra dying of grief if Antony leaves. He begins a mocking description of Cleopatra: "Alack ... her passions are made of nothing but the finest part of pure love," but Antony cuts him short with the news that Fulvia is dead. Stunned at first, Enobarbus recovers and tells Antony that this is cause for rejoicing; now Antony can have Cleopatra. Antony, however, is resolved to leave, and sternly admonishes Enobarbus to stop joking. He will break with Cleopatra and return to Rome, despite Enobarbus' warning that Cleopatra will never survive it. Another reason for returning, Antony explains, is that Sextus Pompeius (usually referred to in the play as Pompey) is threatening to fight a sea-war against Rome; the Roman people are wavering in their allegiance to the Triumvirate, partly because of his, Antony's, refusal to meet his responsibilities.

Comment

Sextus Pompey was the son of Gnaeus Pompey, called Pompey the Great, who with Julius Caesar (adopted father of Octavius Caesar of this play) and Marcus Crassus formed the first Triumvirate. The earlier Pompey and Caesar fell out and made war on each other, and Caesar defeated his rival in the Battle of Pharsalia in 48 B. C. But the son inherited his father's hatred and resentment against Julius Caesar, and his claim to be ruler of the Empire. When Julius Caesar was assassinated, Sextus Pompey took out his grudge against Julius Caesar's heirs, especially his son Octavius.

If he does not act, says Antony, the situation may become dangerous, and he compares it in seriousness to the venom of a serpent.

Comment

Antony receives the news of his wife's death in a truly Roman fashion: unemotional, controlled, in full possession of his feelings. His generous nature is apparent when he praises her as "a great spirit," and the fact that he is an essentially good and moral man is shown by his self-accusation and feelings of guilt, and his wish that he might restore her to life. This is a grave moment, as Antony's Roman feelings assert themselves to dictate that he should make an act of atonement for his past sins. Egypt is beginning to appear to him as essentially the frivolous and wanton place that Philo claimed it to be. Enobarbus plays on the various senses of the word dying, which refers not only to Cleopatra's pretended loss of life but also to the weakness and lassitude which follows sexual intercourse, and, by extension, to the act of intercourse itself. Thus, when he says that Cleopatra "hath such a celerity in dying," he means both that she will make believe that the news of Antony's leaving will kill her, and also that she is a loose woman, quick to indulge in sex and quick to reach a sexual **climax**. The lines about "a serpent's poison" constitute the first of many references to snakes and venom, all leading up to Cleopatra's death by the bite of an asp (a poisonous snake). Another image which will be repeated is contained in Antony's use of the phrase "enchanting queen" to refer to Cleopatra. There will be more references to Cleopatra's power to enchant and bewitch; her powers are part of her connection with Egypt, a land of magic and prophecy (remember the soothsayer), in contrast to the rationalism of the Romans.

SUMMARY

This scene does the following:

1. Through its **imagery**, mainly sexual, it dramatizes the fertility and sexuality with which Egypt and Cleopatra are identified, and which are presided over by Isis, the moon goddess.

2. It shows us a new side of Antony's character: In addition to his weakness for pleasure, he is a moral

man, and he is unable to renounce Rome as easily as he previously wished.

3. It identifies Egypt with the forces of mysticism and magic, in contrast to the Roman faith in reason and free will. It is suggested, by Antony himself, that he is literally under Cleopatra's spell.

4. It complicates the Roman and Egyptian views with which we started, suggesting that they are both inadequate, and that Antony must decide the problem on his own terms.

ACT 1, SCENE 3

The place is the same, a room in Cleopatra's palace. We break in on a tactical discussion between Cleopatra and Charmian, who suspect that Antony is about to leave, but who do not know of Fulvia's death. Cleopatra reveals her feminine tricks and wiles; she sends Charmian to Antony with these instructions: "If you find him sad,/ Say that I am dancing; if in mirth, report/ That I am sudden sick." Charmian counsels her to give in to him, but Cleopatra's strategy is to battle him. Antony enters, and Cleopatra rails at him, simultaneously feigning illness. She postures heroically: "O, never was there a queen/ so mightily betrayed!" She is alternately eloquent - "Eternity was in our lips, and eyes,/ Bliss in our brows' bent," and waspish - "I would I had thy inches," (i.e., his great strength and size, so that she might beat him). Antony vows to go, giving Cleopatra all the reasons except the most important; he speaks of Pompey's rebellion and the civil unrest in Rome. Finally he tells her of Fulvia's death. This provokes from Cleopatra a perverse and unlooked-for reaction: Because Antony is not weeping for his wife, she calls him false, exclaiming, "Now I see, I see,/ In Fulvia's death, how mine received shall be." She then affects illness once more, but continues to rise from her fainting-spells to berate Antony energetically. she accuses him of lying pretense; of using Fulvia's death as a pretext to desert her; and of trying to make his action thus seem honorable. Antony grows angry, and begins to swear, "Now, by my sword - " but Cleopatra interrupts the oath to chide him further, scornfully calling him "this Herculean Roman."

Comment

This is the first, albeit ironical, reference to Antony's patron hero, Hercules, from whom he claimed to be descended. Hercules was a legendary hero or demigod of fabulous size and strength. His life, like Antony's, was checkered with good and bad, triumphing in his very faults and excesses. But above all he was larger than life, of gigantic proportions, and it is this quality which the play endows Antony with.

"O, my oblivion is a very Antony," she sighs, and then, sarcastically, bids him a conventional Roman farewell, to which he, missing the irony, replies in kind.

Comment

The tone of this scene is odd; the issues being argued are very serious, but because Cleopatra's language is witty, and because her posturings border on the absurd, the effect is half-comical. Cleopatra demonstrates here the full range of her emotions and powers of expression; she is by turns witty, serious, shrewish, noble, and wounded. It is this complexity in her character which has led to the disagreement on what kind of woman she really is. Our best course for the moment is to say that she is a woman capable of reconciling all of these disparate qualities; a creature of lightning shifts and a dozen moods. First she illustrates the essential woman in her, coolly mapping her campaign to get the better of Antony. But no sooner has she decided to pretend that she is sick, than she gives in to the temptation to snap at him: "What, says the married woman you may go?" she snarls, blaming him for not making an honest woman of her as he did of Fulvia. Next comes the heroic rhetoric; she is the conventional woman scorned, the innocent, betrayed damsel. But this in turn gives way to what many feel to be her genuinely felt love for Antony, expressed in language of surpassing beauty in the speech beginning "Nay, pray you, seek no colour for your going ..." Here, she has at last attained a truly regal dignity.

Antony replies with all his reasons; the main one, Fulvia's death, comes last, for he fears her reaction to this news. He has reason to; she becomes acid again, and sides with Fulvia against him. He cannot win; had he wept at Fulvia's death, Cleopatra would doubtless have become furious. There is an unconscious **irony** in her lines about his reception of her death. In fact, later in the play, Cleopatra's deaths reported to Antony, and far from treating it with indifference, he kills himself. But he is not indifferent to Fulvia's death either, as Cleopatra claims; he is merely trying to resolve a touchy situation with a woman who can always out-talk him and who has a positive genius for putting him in the wrong. "Cut my lace," she cries, when he lamely resorts to conventional rhetoric himself; she mockingly pretends to be sick and then instantly well, when he haltingly informs her that he loves her, by asking Charmian, in effect, to loosen her stays so that she can breathe as the fit comes over her. Constantly, she throws up to him the fact that the very protestations of love he makes to her are those that he once made to Fulvia. This scene contains the first of many references to Antony's sword, which is symbolic of his military accomplishments and also of his manhood; and it is significant that Cleopatra will not allow him to finish swearing by it, forcing him to leave the word sword ineffectually suspended in mid-air, until she lets it down with, "Upon your sword Sit laurel victory..." Also, for the first time in the play, Cleopatra uses Antony himself as a **metaphor** for sheer size, though she does it ironically: "O, my oblivion is a very Antony ..." We shall encounter this image again.

SUMMARY

This scene:

1. Demonstrates the full range of Cleopatra's personality.

2. Shows dramatically how she casts her spells over Antony.

3. Establishes three new patterns of **imagery**: "the sword," "the world," and "the Herculean hero."

ACT 1, SCENE 4

Now the scene shifts abruptly from Cleopatra's court in Alexandria to the house of Caesar in Rome (where Antony is going): the first of many such far-ranging movements in the action of the play. Caesar has received a letter from the attendant to whom Antony refused to listen in Scene 1. The agent writes that he was unable to deliver the message which Caesar had sent from Rome, and that Antony had shown no concern for his two partners in the Triumvirate. Besides this insult, the agent reports, Antony's idleness and luxury and his constant round of pleasures have taken away his manliness and made him as womanly as Cleopatra. Caesar quotes the letter as evidence to convince Lepidus that their partner in the east has grown soft and rotten. But Lepidus will not be convinced by Caesar's bad opinion. He thinks too highly of Antony to blame him. He says these faults are really only minor compared to his virtues; they are weaknesses which Antony has inherited, not evil habits that he actually chooses.

Comment

This speech by Lepidus does much to characterize him and Antony. It shows us that he wants to remain non-committal toward his partners so as to stay in their good graces. And by saying that Antony is not really responsible for his behavior, he is preparing us to accept Antony's downfall as the result equally of an evil destiny and a guilty will. (In this respect compare Caesar's speech at the end of this scene.)

Caesar will not be put off. Even if Antony's wantonness and carousals are not terrible in themselves, he argues, he has chosen a terrible time to indulge in them. It would be a small matter if Antony were only ruining himself by running around with Cleopatra, but the whole empire is at stake, and he knows it. He is putting his own sensual satisfactions before the welfare of the whole state.

Comment

The danger to which Caesar refers is the rebellion of Pompey; that is why Shakespeare chooses this moment to have the messenger bring news of the conspiracy.

Their conversation is here interrupted by a messenger, a kind of scout that Caesar has sent out to gather news. The information which he brings to the two Triumvirs picks up the subplot of Pompey's growing naval strength. Earlier, Antony had used Pompey's threat as an excuse to leave Cleopatra and return to Rome. We learn that Antony was correct when he estimated the loyalty of the common people. For, the messenger relates, those who never loved Caesar but merely followed him out of fear, are flocking to the seaports to join arms with Pompey when his ships attack. Caesar comments that the loyalty of the crowd is a fickle and a contrary one. They wish for something only until they have it; they do not value a great man until they've lost him.

Comment

Compare Antony's similar sentiment in Scene 2: "Our slippery people,/ Whose love is never link'd to the deserver/ Till his deserts are past …" Though at odds from the beginning, and enemies in deadly earnest at the last, these two men, Antony and Octavius, share the great man's contempt for the common masses and for the fickleness of fate. The waxing and waning of man's fortunate is a central **theme** in this play and in tragedy generally.

The messenger also brings information that Pompey has joined forces with two famous pirates of the Italian coasts, Menecrates and Menas. These two, trafficking in Pompey's name and fearful reputation, have been raiding the maritime provinces of Italy and plundering the coastal trade. This is too much for Caesar. Overcome with distress, he calls aloud on Antony to leave the base pleasure of the Egyptian court and come to Rome's aid. In doing this he tells how, in the old days, Antony was the strongest, manliest soldier of them all.

Comment

This description of Antony's withdrawal from Modena follows Plutarch's account pretty closely. Obviously its purpose here is to raise the audience's admiration for Antony by showing how great and how austere a soldier he had been in the past. Shakespeare must keep his balance in describing the tragic hero. He cannot make Antony too good or we will be angry at the injustice of his tragic fate; he cannot make him totally evil or we will not be able to admire him enough to feel sorry for him when he dies. Since we have last seen Antony resolved to do his duty as a Roman (Scene 3), and since this scene ends by praising him, we feel at this point that in our eyes he has returned to his former stature.

The scene ends as Caesar and Lepidus prepare a council of war to decide how best to defeat Pompey.

SUMMARY

This scene is important because:

1. It introduces Antony's fellow Triumvirs, Octavius Caesar and Lepidus.

2. It shows Caesar's anger at Antony's conduct in Egypt.

3. It brings us up to date on Sextus Pompeius's planned naval attack by showing that some famous pirates and the common people have gone to his support.

4. It describes the noble character of Antony before he fell in love with Cleopatra.

ACT 1, SCENE 5

Scene 5 returns to Cleopatra's palace Alexandria. The Egyptian queen, surrounded by her attendants, complains of how much she misses her lover. She asks Charmian to give her a sedative, a kind of sleeping potion, so she can forget her loneliness in sleep. But she is not so sad that she cannot joke with her eunuch, Mardian, about his sexual impotence. She tells him to be glad he has no sexual desires which would make him long for someone as she does. He replies that while he might never perform the sexual act, he can dream about it. He has erotic thoughts about the adultery of Venus (goddess of love and wife of Vulcan) and Mars (god of war). Cleopatra tries to picture Antony in his absence, recalling his physical presence when he made love to her.

Comment

She calls him "the arm/ And burgonet of men." "Arm" here means sword, as "burgonet" means helmet. This supports the "sword" pattern of **imagery** of Scene 3. Mardian's mention of Venus and Mars may be a sly reference to Cleopatra and Antony.

Her thought of Antony's strength and manly prime leads her to contrast her own aging charms and she begins to doubt she can hold so great a man. She sees her Egyptian skin as burnt black from the sun and wrinkled with age. (Shakespeare obviously thought of Cleopatra as negroid, rather than the Greek she actually was.) She recalls, almost nostalgically, how her youthful beauty had conquered the hearts of the great Roman conquerors Julius Caesar and Pompey the Great (the father of the Sextus Pompeius of this story).

Comment

This passage contains one of several references to Cleopatra's age. Shakespeare wants to characterize the great queen as past her prime, her beauty somewhat faded. She must rely more and more on artifice and feminine wiles to attract her lover. While age makes Cleopatra more wily, however, it makes her more tragic and sympathetic to the audience.

Here Alexas, another of Cleopatra's attendants, enters with a message from Antony. The joy of hearing from him reassures her, lifts the gloom which had begun to thicken about her. She is impatient to hear his greeting and to find out how he looked when he gave it. Alexas hands her a pearl which Antony had kissed before sending, as his token of the kingdoms he will conquer for her. She is not surprised to hear that his disposition and demeanor were temperate when he sent it.

Comment

In Cleopatra's eyes, Antony can do no wrong. When she discovers that he was neither sad nor merry, but between both, she praises him: not sad, for he must inspire his troops with optimism: not merry, because he missed her. But had he been either, she would praise him equally: "Be'st thou sad or merry,/ The violence of either thee becomes,/ So does it no man else."

Immediately the queen, like a young girl in love again, sits down to answer Antony's message. Her mind goes back to her former Roman lover for a second, and she asks her maid, Charmian, "Did I .../ Ever love Caesar so?" And the maid taunts her by mimicking her former praises of Caesar when she was in love with him: "O that brave Caesar!" and "The valiant Caesar!"

At this Cleopatra threatens to bloody her teeth. For she praised Caesar in her "salad days," when she was young and ignorant, she says: "green in judgment: cold in blood."

SUMMARY

This slight scene is introduced to tell us more about Cleopatra's character. We have seen her before always relating to Antony; now we see her true self when he is away. The effect is to make Cleopatra seem erotic by nature and not simply as a means to seduce Antony. She is genuinely in love with him but not completely sure of being able to keep him in his absence. Her mention of "salad days" is another indirect reference to her age.

ANTONY AND CLEOPATRA

TEXTUAL ANALYSIS

ACT 2: SCENES 1 - 4

ACT 2 SCENE 1

From Cleopatra's court in Alexandria we move back to Messina, in Sicily, where Pompey has his headquarters. (Remember, there were originally no Act divisions in the play.) There, in Messina, Pompey with the pirates Menecrates and Menas (mentioned earlier in Act 1, Scene 4) plans his rebellion against the Triumvirate. Pompey is unhappy because of the delay in their plan. He feels that the longer they wait, the worse will become the Roman State for which they are going to fight. Menecrates, however, calms him by saying that the delay may all be for the best; it is in the hands of the gods. Then Pompey analyzes their chances in the forthcoming battle and describes the characters and weaknesses of their foes. His chances are good, he estimates. His navy holds mastery of the sea, and the common people of Italy have swung to his side. Besides, Mark Antony is away in Egypt, too caught up in court pleasures and intrigues to care about larger affairs. Octavius Caesar controls the purses of the citizens, but cannot control their love. And Lepidus is a weak sister: he keeps in the others' good graces, and they in his, but there is no love lost among them. Pompey realizes that the success of their plan depends upon the great warrior, Antony, remaining in Egypt; so much so that he apostrophizes (as Caesar did to Antony is Scene 4 of Act 1) to Cleopatra to keep Antony with her by means of her witchcraft and beauty. Pompey hopes that Antony, with his sense of honor dulled by sensual indulgence, will not come to aid his friends.

> Comment

Here again Cleopatra's age is referred to. "Soften thy waned lip!" Pompey exhorts her, implying that her lip is withered or faded with age.

So Varrius' entrance at this point is very dramatic. Just as Pompey finishes wishing that Antony would stay in Egypt to insure their success, Varrius brings news that he has already left Egypt and is expected at any moment in Rome.

> Comment

Note how great a reputation Antony has as a warrior, even among his enemies.

At first Pompey cannot believe it; but immediately he tries to take courage by saying that their conspiracy must be a grave threat indeed if Antony will leave Cleopatra just to fight against them. Menas is also shaken up by the news. He tries to find some comfort in the hope that Caesar and Antony may fall out with one another, since both Antony's wife and brother had formerly warred with Caesar. Pompey agrees that all is not right among the Triumvirs, but fears they might be able to overlook their own petty squabbles long enough to unite against the conspirators. At any rate, he will not fall victim to wishful thinking. Laying the outcome in the hands of the gods, he nevertheless bluffly counsels his friends "to use our strongest hands."

SUMMARY

The main purposes of this scene have been:

1. To introduce the conspirators, and to further the subplot of their conspiracy.

2. To provide an objective analysis of the characters of the Triumvirs and their mutual relationships.

3. To show what fear Antony's arrival in Rome inspires in the conspirators.

ACT 2 SCENE 2

In the house of the third and weakest of the Triumvirs, Lepidus, Antony and Caesar's arrival is expected. Lepidus opens the scene by trying to persuade Enobarbus to use his influence on his friend and captain to greet Caesar with "soft and gentle speech," so as not to offend him and stir up ill-feeling among the Triumvirs. For Lepidus realizes that the three leaders must suppress their own quarrels with each other in order to pursue their common quarrel against Pompey successfully: only in their unity is their strength. Enobarbus has just refused Lepidus' request absolutely, when the two disgruntled leaders enter with their parties. With Antony is his lieutenant, Ventidius; with Caesar, his shrewd and politic adviser, Agrippa, and the wealthy patron of the arts, Maecenas. Both parties are absorbed in conversation. Lepidus immediately tries to buffer and soften the collision between the two by admonishing them not to let passions or hard words turn their trivial differences into a bitter fight, lest "we do commit murder in healing wounds."

Comment

The role of peacemaker is characteristic of Lepidus not only in this scene but throughout the play. Remember, it was he who stood up for Antony Against Caesar's condemnation in Act 1, Scene 4. In fact, it is his lack of passion which is responsible in part for his own downfall.

Antony is the first to agree; he embraces Caesar, who welcomes him to Rome. But their show of friendliness is only on the surface; beneath it the old resentments rankle. Antony opens the conversation by telling Caesar, in effect, to mind his own business. What he, Antony, does in his own province (the East and, therefore, Egypt) is his own affair and no concern of Caesar's. Caesar denies having meddled, says that he does not criticize Antony's conduct in Egypt, but his conspiracy in Rome. He accuses his partner of having an interest in, or at least being the excuse for, the wars which his late wife, Fulvia, and his brother, Lucius, had waged against the Roman state. Antony pleads innocent to the charge, and claims he has reports from among Caesar's own troops that Lucius, in challenging Caesar's authority, challenged his own brother's as well. He put himself on Caesar's side of the dispute and assured his partner of it by means of letters at the time. To question his loyalty now, at this late date, is only to pick a fight: any old stick will do to beat a dog, as it were. Antony's accusation hurts Caesar - "You praise yourself,/ By laying defects of judgment to me," Caesar says - and when the dispute threatens to break down into a personal squabble, Antony tries to keep the atmosphere cool. He first flatters Caesar with a gentle compliment on his good judgment of men and events, and then turns Fulvia's indiscretion into a joke at his own expense. Caesar is too astute not to be confident of Antony's loyalty, he says. And even Caesar himself, master of a third of the world, would have had his hands full taming Antony's spirited wife. After this note of humor Caesar breaks off and tries a new line of argument. He accuses Antony of disregarding his official letters and insulting his messenger.

Comment

This refers to Antony's dismissal of the messenger in Act 1, Scene 1, which Caesar considered an insult to himself.

Antony admits the incident but claims innocence of any insult intended, for two reasons: (1) the messenger overstepped himself by entering his chamber uninvited; and (2) he had a hangover that morning that soured his disposition. Besides, the next day he as much as asked the fellow's pardon. Again he accuses Caesar of patching a quarrel out of trivial slights that do not really matter. Get to the point, he says. This time Caesar is hurt by the accusation into his sharpest attack so far. Before, he had questioned, first, Antony's loyalty, and then his manners; now he attacks his honor by accusing Antony of having broken his promise to lend arms and aid when Caesar needed them to fight Fulvia and Lucius. This is the heart of Caesar's grievance, and Lepidus is alarmed, for it is a most serious charge. But Antony answers it calmly. He had not denied Caesar's requests but only neglected them, because he was so caught up in the pleasures of Cleopatra's court. It was to lure him out of Egypt and away from Cleopatra that Fulvia instigated the war against Rome. He asks Caesar's pardon, not for having intended any injury, but for having been "the ignorant motive" of it. At this concession the entire company are relieved and relax a bit. Lepidus praises Antony's nobility; Maecenas begs them to break off their dispute; even Enobarbus (despite what he said to Lepidus at the beginning of the scene) oversteps his place and advises the two leaders to turn their quarrel toward Pompey. Antony promptly rebukes him for it. Now it is Caesar's turn for concession, and he backs out of the argument neatly by claiming that he does not so much dislike what Antony says, as the way in which he says it. He would adopt any means, he vows, to strengthen their friendship and insure the unity of their dominion over the entire world. This is the cue for Caesar's calculating adviser, Agrippa, to put forth his plan for bringing the two quarreling leaders back together again. Caesar has a sister, Octavia, he says, and Antony is now a widower.

Comment

Plutarch tells us that Octavia was the eldest sister of Caesar, really his half-sister, by the same father, and had been "left the widow of her first husband Caius Marcellus, who dyed not long before …"

Let their marriage, Agrippa urges, be the knot that ties the two Triumvirs perpetually together. The match would be perfect: She is beautiful and virtuous; he is "the best of men." Their marriage would cool all jealousies, squelch all fears, scotch all rumors that threatened to divide the Triumvirate, while, as Caesar's sister, she would be the intercessor and mediator between the two. They receive his suggestion cautiously at first. Caesar is unsure whether Antony considers Cleopatra his mistress or his wife. But after they are sure of each other's acceptance their enthusiasm grows. Antony grasps Caesar's hand in friendship and swears brotherhood and loyalty, which Caesar returns. Then the two immediately fall to talking about the conspiracy of Pompey. Antony is awkward about defying the rebel leader. He feels obliged to repay certain "strange courtesies" which Pompey has lately lavished on him before he can openly quarrel with the rebels.

Comment

We have seen - Act 1, Scene 1 - how afraid the conspirators were of Antony's military power. No doubt they have been "buttering him up" to keep him friendly and out of their quarrel with Caesar and Lepidus.

But time is pressing, Lepidus urges. Pompey's naval strength is second to none, and his land forces grow stronger daily. The three Triumvirs decide to seek a meeting with Pompey at his camp near Mt. Misenum, but first proceed to Caesar's house to settle the business of Antony's marriage to Octavia.

Comment

This marks the end of the Roman atmosphere of the scene. Antony has argued straightforwardly and convincingly; he has shown himself more than a match for Octavius. He has, finally, in accepting the offer of Octavia in marriage, demonstrated his sobriety, his sense of responsibility and his loyalty to Rome.

When they depart, Enobarbus, Agrippa and Maecenas remain alone on stage. The two Roman statesmen welcome the soldier back from Egypt and pump him for information and descriptions of Cleopatra's fabulous court. He not only vouches for the truth of their most fantastic stories about its luxury, but goes them one better in his sumptuous description of Cleopatra's arrival in Cilicia to appear before Antony's tribunal.

Comment

This speech gives us a good example of one of the ways in which Shakespeare borrowed from his sources. He takes not only his story or plot and his characters from Plutarch, but even some of his speeches as well. Here he puts into **blank verse** this description which comes out of North's translation of Plutarch:

"... she disdained to set forward otherwise, but to take her barge in the river of Cydnus, the poop whereof was of gold, the sails of purple, and the oars of silver, which kept stroke in rowing after the sound of music of flutes, howboys, citherns, viols, and such other instruments as they played upon in the barge. And now for the person of herself: she was laid under a pavilion of cloth of gold of tissue, appareled and attired like the goddess Venus commonly drawn in picture: and hard by her, on either hand of her, pretty fair boys appareled as painters do set forth god Cupid, with little fans in their hands, with the which they fanned wind upon her. Her ladies and gentlewomen also, the fairest of them were appareled like the nymphs Nereids (which are the mermaids of the waters) and like the Graces, some steering the helm, others tending the tackle and ropes of the barge, out of the which there came a wonderful passing sweet savor of perfumes, that perfumed the wharf's side, pestered with innumerable multitudes of people. Some of them followed the barge all alongst the river-side: others also ran out of the city to see her coming in. So that in the end there ran such multitudes of people one after another to see her, that Antonius was left post alone in the market-place in his imperial seat to give audience: and there went a rumor in the people's mouths, that the goddess Venus was come to play with the god Bacchus, for the general good of all Asia. When Cleopatra landed, Antonius sent to invite her to supper to him. But she sent word again, he should do better rather to come and sup with her."

Called before Antony to answer charges that she had supported Cassius and Brutus against him in the battle of Philippi, Cleopatra plans to escape his inquisition and reprisals by making him fall in love with her. That accounts for her spectacular arrival by boat on the River Cydnus. And what a boat! Its poop (a partial deck raised above the main deck in the rear) was fashioned of solid gold. The oars which propelled it were of silver, and they kept stroke to the music of flutes on board (as soldiers, for example, march to the sound of drums and martial music). The sails were purple and perfumed so that the very breeze languished and grew lovesick in breathing on them, and their scent assailed the spectators who lined the river banks to watch.

Comment

Purple dye, sometimes called Tyrian purple, was made from the shells of certain mollusks. Because of its richness and its rareness it was considered the color of kings and queens in ancient times. That Cleopatra should use this to color her sails is a sign, like the golden deck, silver oars, etc., of fabulous wealth and wasteful extravagance.

The rigging and tackle were of silk, as befitted the softness of the ship's "hands," Cleopatra's attendants, who resembled so many mermaids or nereids (mythical water nymphs, daughters of the sea-god Nereus) as they managed the ship and fawned over its cargo, Cleopatra. Cleopatra herself was stunning beyond description. She neither stood nor sat, but reclined (probably on the golden poop deck), shaded by a sumptuous silken canopy into whose tissue were woven threads of purest gold. She resembled a painting of the Goddess of Love herself (probably the lost Venus Anadyomene, or "Venus Rising out of the Sea," painted by the Greek, Apelles, in the 4th century B. C.), only more lovely, surrounded by pretty young boys, who stirred the perfumed air about her with many-colored fans, like so many little cupids (Cupid was the son of Venus by Mars, God of War).

Comment

Some critics have this speech inappropriate in the mouth of the Roman soldier, Enobarbus. Its lush and sensual descriptions, its lavish use of imagination, its classical and mythological references are out of place coming from the usually straightforward, prosaic, and even vulgar Enobarbus. On the other hand, that contrast between Rome and the mysterious East is just what Shakespeare wanted. Even Enobarbus is overcome by Cleopatra's charms.

Word of the spectacle soon emptied the city as the people flocked to the river banks to watch, leaving Antony by himself in the market place, enthroned for his tribunals, "whistling to the air." He sent word to invite the queen to dinner with him: she refused his offer but returned the invitation, which he accepted. And there at the banquet Antony lost his heart to her.

Comment

Shakespeare seems to be confused about when and where Antony first saw and fell in love with Cleopatra. In line 187 Enobarbus says that "she pursed up his heart upon the river of Cydnus," but later in Scene 2, 214-216 that "Antony/ Enthroned in a market-place, did sit alone," all the while. It was only later that night, at her feast, that he first saw her and fell in love.

Agrippa and Enobarbus then exchange stories of Cleopatra's fabulous beauty which could bewitch great (Julius) Caesar, and which is made even more perfect by every defect in it. So when Maecenas says that Antony, pledged to Octavia, must give up Cleopatra for good, Enobarbus answers: "Never; he will not."

Comment

With this answer, Enobarbus brings out into the open his suspicion that the proposed marriage may not succeed in its purpose of uniting the two Triumvirs, if Octavia cannot overcome Antony's love for Cleopatra. Note also Enobarbus's reference to Cleopatra's advancing years - "Age cannot wither her" - which he discounts as a possible reason why Antony might have grown tired or jaded with his queen.

The scene ends on Maecenas' earnest, but somewhat hollow, hope that Octavia's "beauty, wisdom, modesty, can settle the heart of Antony," and reform the notorious rogue.

SUMMARY

This scene contains several important developments which can be divided into two distinct groups. Part one of the scene has a noticeable "Roman" atmosphere, and is dominated by Antony. It is developed in three stages:

1. The encounter between Antony and Caesar, and their argument.

2. The resolution of the argument and the plan to marry Octavia to Antony.

3. The decision of the Triumvirs to unite their forces against Pompey. Part two takes on an "Egyptian" coloring from Enobarbus' detailed description of Cleopatra, who dominates his conversation with the Roman statesmen. Shakespeare puts the two parts side by side to heighten the contrast between Roman rationality and Egyptian sensuality, which are also the two warring sides of Antony's nature. The **climax** of the scene is reached when Enobarbus and Agrippa raise the question of which side Antony will finally choose: Octavia or Cleopatra.

ACT 2, SCENE 3

The conversation among Enobarbus and Caesar's counselors provides the time needed between the departure of the Triumvirs from Lepidus' house and their arrival at Caesar's. (Although Antony insisted upon Lepidus' accompanying them to visit Octavia, Lepidus does not appear with them in this scene at Caesar's house.) The scene opens with Antony's saying good-bye to Caesar and Octavia. In parting, he forewarns his prospective wife that, after their marriage, he will be away from her often on military and political adventures. She accepts this and promises that she will be on her knees all the while he is gone, praying constantly for him.

Comment

Shakespeare contrasts the "beauty, wisdom, modesty" that Octavia reveals here with the "infinite variety" of Cleopatra described by Enobarbus in the scene just before. "Vilest things/ Become themselves," in the Egyptian queen, so that "the holy priests/ Bless her, when she's riggish (wanton). (Act 2, Scene 2, ll. 238 ff.) The effect is to make Antony's betrayal of Octovia almost certain.

No sooner are the sister and brother gone, when the soothsayer, who comes from Cleopatra's court and who reminds us of the magic and the mystery of the East, appears to tell Antony's fortune and to prophesy how his new friendship and alliance will turn out. Badly, the wizard tells him, and urges Antony to return at once to Egypt. For Antony's guiding spirit or guardian angel is greater than Caesar's when he is alone, but when they are together, it is overpowered; he suffers always by comparison with the younger man. His luck always deserts him; in games with Caesar, he is sure to lose.

Comment

The fortune teller's prophecy is a true one. In this speech we get a forewarning of the final outcome of the play, when Caesar will defeat Antony once again. Then the game will be war; and the stakes they play for will be the entire world and even life itself.

Antony is so struck by the soothsayer's advice, that he makes him promise not to repeat his prophecy to anyone else. He sends the soothsayer off to tell Ventidius, his lieutenant, that he wants to see him. When the wiseman is gone, Antony confirms his prophecy as true in a short soliloquy (a speech in which a character, usually alone, speaks his thoughts aloud to the audience, no one else on stage overhearing him). In his gambling with Caesar, Antony admits, the dice have always betrayed him; in sports, luck has been with his rival. He then makes a startling decision: he will follow the soothsayer's advice, and even while tying the marriage knot with Octavia, he vows he will return to Egypt to continue his affair with Cleopatra. "I make this marriage for my peace," he says, "In the East my pleasure lies."

Comment

Antony is like the prize in a tug-of-war between Rome and Egypt. To show this, Shakespeare alternates scenes in which Antony's sense of honor and duty to Octavia pulls him toward Rome with others in which Egypt and Cleopatra draw him toward love - and doom. In this scene the question of who will win, raised by Enobarbus and Agrippa in Act 2, Scene 2, is answered. Cleopatra wins. Antony, after promising faithfulness to Octavia and begging her trust, turns around and violates that trust in favor of his Egyptian mistress. He is only using Caesar's sister for political purposes.

Antony's business with Ventidius is short: he gives his lieutenant orders to report to Parthia to check the enemy invasion there.

Comment

The expedition to Parthia was to defeat the armies of Labienus, who had been conquering all of Asia and invading the territory over which Antony was supposed to rule. The invasion is spoken of earlier in Act 1, Scene 2, ll. 96 ff.

SUMMARY

This scene though short is decisive for Antony's fate. It contains the following developments:

1. Introduces Caesar's sister Octavia, whom Antony has promised to marry, and contrasts her with Cleopatra.

2. In the fortune teller's prophecy we get an inkling of Antony's future defeat at the hands of Caesar.

3. Right after he has promised Octavia that he will reform his conduct in the future so as to act "by the rule," Antony decides to return to Cleopatra. This shows him to be two-faced, a slave to his own weaknesses and baser appetites.

4. His commission to Ventidius picks up the story of Labienus's invasion in Parthia and ties his lieutenant more closely into the action of the play.

ACT 2, SCENE 4

Scene 4 is very short, ten lines of dialogue between Lepidus, Maecenas, and Agrippa to show the Romans marshaling their forces for the confrontation, several days later, with Pompey at Mt. Misenum.

ANTONY AND CLEOPATRA

TEXTUAL ANALYSIS

ACT 2: SCENES 5 - 7

ACT 2, SCENE 5

This scene whisks us back to Cleopatra's palace in Alexandria. The queen is restless, love-sick, longing for her absent Antony. To pass the time she first calls for music, "the food of love," but when Mardian, her eunuch, enters to play for her, she dismisses him and challenges her maid, Charmian, to shoot a game of billiards with her instead. Charmian declines, but Mardian takes up the challenge, and Cleopatra, with an obvious sexual jest, says she may as well play games with a eunuch as with a woman. She never gets to the game, however, for already her quicksilver mood has shifted again, and she wishes to go fishing. With every fish she catches she will pretend she is drawing home her roving lover. Charmian reminds her of a trick she once played on Antony.

Comment

Plutarch tells the whole story. Out fishing once, with Cleopatra nearby, Antony wanted to show off but could catch no fish. So he ordered some fisherman, when he dropped in his line, to dive under, unnoticed, and attach a fish to his hook. In this way he pulled in two or three fish. Cleopatra saw through his ruse but did not let on, and next day when he was fishing again she had one of her own divers attach an old salted fish - i.e., one that has been aged and preserved in salt a long time - to his hook, which he then pulled in to the laughter of all.

And Cleopatra reminisces about the wonderful times she had with Antony, including one in which, both drunk, she dressed him in her woman's garments while she "wore his sword Phillipan."

Comment

Shakespeare mentions their exchange of clothes here as a sign of weakness and effeminacy which overcame Antony in Egypt. Her wearing his sword continues the "sword" pattern of **imagery**. As the sign or emblem of Antony's manliness, it shows that she had assumed the masculine role. The fact that it was the sword he used to defeat Brutus and Cassius in the battle of Philippi (and, hence, named after it), when he was at the peak of his glory and strength, deepens the irony.

But her laughter is suddenly stilled by the appearance of a messenger from Italy. Immediately she jumps to conclusions: "Antonius dead!" she screams, and alternately threatens and cajoles the messenger to give her good news, as though by promising gold or threatening death she could make his message any different from what it is. Continually interrupted by her gifts and threats, the messenger can only give his news piecemeal. Antony is well, he says, and friends with Caesar, and adds darkly, "Caesar, and he, are greater friends than ever" - but does not yet reveal the reason and seal of this friendship. Cleopatra is overjoyed, and over generous - "Make thee a fortune from me" - until the messenger's "But yet, madam ..." gives her first real reason to suspect something is wrong. She snatches at it immediately, but still does not catch the messenger's drift when he says, "he's bound unto Octavia." Why? For what purposes, she asks, and only slowly does the shock of despair overcome her when he replies, "Madam, he's married to Octavia." Once the truth is clear and out in the open, she reacts immediately and violently. Suddenly she is upon him, knocks him to the ground, cursing him and, despite his protests, kicking and scratching. She threatens to put out his eyes, tear out his hair, have him whipped with wire and boiled in brine. Then in an instant she relents, all softness again, begging him only to say it is not so to make his fortune. When he sticks by his message, she is at his throat once more, this time with a knife, and would have his life but that he runs away. Charmian tries to calm her when he is gone, and succeeds enough to have Cleopatra call the boy back again.

Comment

She lives up to her name, "Serpent of old Nile." She is thinking of herself as a serpent when after uttering the curse, "kindly creatures/ Turn all to serpents!" she says of herself, "Though I am mad, I will not bite him."

But the boy is afraid to come before the "fury of a woman scorned," and his fear awakens a spark of nobility and self-respect in Cleopatra. She regrets having struck the messenger for two reasons: (1) he is socially inferior to her and therefore she demeans herself by hitting him; (2) it is not his fault, but rather her own that Antony's marriage upsets her. In a sort of half-apology, she advises the boy when he reappears, to tell good tidings but let bad tidings tell themselves, and asks him again if Antony is married. When he confirms the news once more, once more she flies into a rage, over and over demanding that he repeat the bitter news and then cursing him for it when he does. However, she will not lay hands on him again, but banishes him from her presence. Her panic recedes with her violence. She begins to recover her wits, and though her heart is breaking, she is already weaving the snares and trammels that will snatch her lover out of his new wife's arms and fetch him back to hers. But first she must size her rival up. She sends Alexas to speak to the messenger to find out what Antony's wife looks like: how old she is, her temperament or disposition, the color of her hair, how tall she is. Then she asks her waiting-woman Charmian to pity her in silence and lead her to bed.

Comment

Though Cleopatra is broken-hearted at Antony's seeming rejection of her, she is so because she still loves him. Hence she is torn between two courses of action: (1) to abandon him to Octavia as a Gorgon (a mythological demon, Medusa, whose scalp was covered with snakes instead of hair and whose sight turned men to stone); or, to try to win him back as a Mars (Roman God of War). The description of Antony as both Gorgon and Mars is a **metaphor** based on a kind of Elizabethan painting called a perspective, which showed two or three different pictures according to the angle from which one viewed it. She is saying that Antony is like such a picture; from one point of view he is hateful, from another lovable.

SUMMARY

As in most of the Egyptian scenes, Shakespeare has really nothing new - neither action, nor piece of information, nor plot development - to tell us. Yet he must switch back to Cleopatra's court every so often to keep her image fresh in our minds. Sometimes he does this merely by having a character describe the court life (Enobarbus in Act 2, Scene 2) or by having some representative of the East (the soothsayer, Act 2, Scene 3) appear on stage. Here, as in the last scene that took place in Egypt (Act 1, Scene 5), he shows us a messenger bringing news to Cleopatra from Antony, only this time the news is disturbing. But the purpose and construction of the scene is the same. There is the preliminary conversation between the queen and her attendant, the joking (always including some sexual jest), the memories, all of which reveal Cleopatra's love-sickness and longing. Then comes the messenger whom she impatiently duns for his news. And, finally, her reaction to the news. Therefore, the purpose of the scene is twofold:

1. To strengthen the image of the mysterious and sensual East and to maintain its balance over the moral and rational West.

2. To deepen the characterization of Cleopatra, in particular by revealing some of "her infinite variety," the impetuosity of her actions, her quicksilver moods, her cunning and scheming, and last but not least her devotion to Antony.

| ACT 2, SCENE 6

Now comes the long-expected confrontation between the Triumvirs and the conspirators near Mt. Misenum in Naples. The two sides have exchanged hostages as pledges of their good intent, and the Triumvirs have sent Pompey terms for an armistice before the armies start to fight. Now Caesar starts negotiations by asking Pompey if he will accept their terms for a truce. Pompey replies by stating the reasons for his rebellion. Just as the Triumvirs-Caesar's adopted son Octavius and close friends - avenged Julius Caesar's murder by defeating Brutus and Cassius, his murderers, at the battle of Philippi: so he, Sextus Pompey, with his friends, will overthrow the Triumvirs in order to avenge his father, Pompey the Great, whom Julius Caesar had overthrown.

Comment

Julius Caesar defeated his fellow soldier and rival, Gnaeus Pompey, in the battle of Pharsalia in 48 B. C. Pompey was later murdered in Egypt.

That is his personal grudge against the Triumvirs; his public purpose is to do what Brutus did in killing Julius Caesar: to rid Rome of an oppressive tyranny and return the people to their freedom. His aggressive statement puts Antony's hackles up, who challenges him to a sea contest, since he will not face the Triumvirs' superior forces on land, Pompey replies with a sarcastic jibe that Antony had bought his father's house (Pompey the Great's) at auction and then refused to pay for it.

Comment

The connection between Antony's vaunting challenge and Pompey's jibing reply is the word "over-count." Antony says his land armies "over-count" or outnumber Pompey's. Pompey uses the same word to mean "cheat" - You have cheated me of my father's house.

As the exchange becomes heated, Lepidus, the peacemaker, steps in to cool the atmosphere. He asks Pompey to answer Caesar's question - does he accept the truce or not? Antony is quick to remark that they are not begging him, and Caesar adds that it will be for his own good. Then Pompey repeats the terms of the treaty: In return for rule over Sicily and Sardinia (another large island in the Mediterranean off the west coast of Italy), he must promise to rid all the Mediterranean Sea of pirates and to pay an annual tax to Rome in the form of wheat.

Comment

We have seen how Pompey has been using the support of the notorious pirates Menas and Menecrates to raid the Italian coastal towns and prey upon shipping (Act 1, Scene 4, 11. 48 ff; Act 2, Scene 1).

This agreed upon, the two armies will pull back without fighting. "Know, then," he says,, "I came before you here a man prepared/ To take this offer. But Mark Anthony/ Put me to some impatience." He feels he deserved better from the Roman general because he had welcomed Antony's mother and given her protection in Sicily when she was forced to flee from Italy, after her son Lucius's rebellion was defeated. Antony acknowledges the debt of friendship, and Pompey, grasping his hand, says he is surprised to see Antony at all, this far from Egypt. "The beds in the East are soft," Antony acknowledges, but duty has called him away from pleasure, "thanks to you." Then Pompey concludes the business of their meeting by asking that the terms of the treaty be written up and sealed.

Comment

Pompey offers only a show of resistance to the truce, and is quick to avoid a fight because of the unexpected return of Antony and the seeming friendliness of the Triumvirs. Remember, the rebels had hoped that the three would squabble and break apart (Act 2, Scene 1).

The pact will be sealed with a celebration party thrown by each of the four signers. Pompey offers to choose lots to decide who will begin. Antony wants the honor of being first, but Pompey repeats that they must choose lots. But whether first or last, he taunts Antony, your "fine Egyptian cookery shall have/ The fame." Did not Julius Caesar get fat on it? Antony stiffens at the remark. But Pompey assures him, disarmingly, "I have fair meanings, sir."

Comment

We know Pompey's feelings about Julius Caesar; he hated him for having deposed his father. We also know that the Triumvirs were friends of the first Caesar and revenged his death. It is no wonder, then, that when Pompey mentions his name jokingly, Antony should resent it, and no doubt that Pompey intended this. The peace they have just agreed to will be an uneasy one.

Pompey continues to rib Antony. Now he includes Cleopatra in the joke by referring to a famous **episode**, in which one of her friends, Apollodorus, carried the queen to Caesar wrapped in a mattress.

> Comment

Plutarch gives this account, Caesar had secretly sent for Cleopatra, but when she had come to his palace she could find no way to enter without being seen. So she had Apollodorus wrap her in a kind of quilt or blanket and smuggle her in on his back.

Enobarbus finishes the story that Pompey starts and draws from the rebel leader a handshake, an offer of friendship, and praise for his qualities as a fighter. The straightforward soldier returns the compliment, though not the love, he says, and this openness even further ingratiates him with Pompey. Then Pompey with a flourish invites everyone at the parley to celebrate their treaty aboard his flagship, and all leave but Enobarbus and Menas, the pirate. Menas first speaks an aside in which he shows his apprehension over the new treaty: "Thy father, Pompey, would never have made this treaty."

> Comment

An aside, unlike a soliloquy, is spoken when other characters are on stage and may be heard by them also. So it is much shorter than a soliloquy, and its purpose is not to explore character or provide motivation, but to awaken the audience's fear or arouse its curiosity.

Then Menas addresses Enobarbus before he can leave with the rest and falls into conversation with him. There is no pretense between the two; each recognizes the other for what he is: a thief. Menas makes his living as a pirate; Enobarbus as a mercenary (a soldier of fortune, who sells his services to the highest bidder and fights for pay, not patriotism). They shake hands and exchange roguish pleasantries until the conversation gets around to the present situation. "We came hither to fight with you," Enobarbus says, and Menas answers that he is sorry the battle did not come off. He distrusts the truce, he confides to his erstwhile enemy, and feels that "Pompey doth this day laugh away his fortune." Then Menas, surprised at seeing Antony back in Italy, brings up the subject of Cleopatra. This is Enobarbus' cue to blurt out the marriage plans between Antony and Octavia. But he does not agree with Menas that this will insure the continued friendship of Caesar and Antony. Just the opposite, this nuptial band that was supposed to bind the two together will turn out to be the rope that strangles their friendship. "Octavia is of a holy, cold, and still conversation (behavior)"; Antony is not. And Enobarbus predicts that Antony "will to his Egyptian dish again: then shall the sighs of Octavia blow the fire up in Caesar," and the marriage which was intended to bind the Triumvirate together will break it apart. Menas then suggests they go on to the party to drink each other's health, and Enobarbus accepts, saying, "we have used our throats in Egypt."

Comment

The feeling of confidence between the two which Shakespeare establishes early in the scene is necessary later on. We could not otherwise expect these men, enemies until just a few moments before, to speak so frankly and openly about their feelings toward their leaders. But that is just what Menas is after. Recall that it was Menas, in Act 2, Scene 1, who hoped the alliance between Caesar and Antony would dissolve when Antony came home. Here he pumps Enobarbus for some clue that may prove his hope true. To win the soldier's confidence, the pirate confides his own distrust of the new treaty. And when he has the information he wants, he breaks off the conversation.

SUMMARY

This scene produces three important developments:

1. The treaty with Pompey avoids a showdown fight for the time being and allows Antony to turn his attention to his Eastern empire and Cleopatra.

2. Menas's distrust of the treaty and the hard feelings between its signers make us suspect that it will be short-lived.

3. Enobarbus puts into words the suspicion held by all that not only will Antony's marriage not close the rift between him and Caesar, but will actually widen it instead.

ACT 2, SCENE 7

This scene takes place soon after the last. Everyone has gone aboard Pompey's galley for the feast; they have eaten and drunk, and now it is time for the "banquet" or dessert. Two or three servingmen bring it on stage and chat and joke for a minute to set the scene. Their joking reveals that the party has been a success; the revelers are in different stages of drunkenness, and Lepidus in particular is flushed with his drinks. As the peacemaker, he tried to relax the tension building up between the two groups at the party and did this by encouraging them to drown their enmity in wine. When they became quarrelsome he would break it up by offering them a drink - and having one himself. Since he cannot hold his liquor as well as the others he has succeeded only in losing all sense of discretion. One of the servants observes that Lepidus has a name only among his companions; he is not their equal or fellow as a man. As useless to be too small for a job as too great; a reed is as useless in battle as a sword that is too heavy to wield, he reflects. His friend agrees: to have a job that one cannot do is like having empty sockets where eyes should be.

Comment

The servant's lines contain two metaphors. "To be called into a huge sphere, and not to be seen to move in it, are the holes where eyes should be, which pitifully disaster the cheeks." The reference to eyes is obvious; however, hidden in the language is a less obvious **metaphor** based on the stars. The words "sphere," "move," and "disaster" point the reference. Besides meaning "place in life," or "ruling circle," "sphere" refers to the Ptolemaic system of astronomy, which from ancient times was used to describe the movements of heavenly bodies. Hence the second meaning of "move" refers to the observed movements of the stars. Ptolemy taught that the planets and stars were the visible parts of seven hollow spheres which surrounded the earth concentrically (i.e., one sphere or hollow ball inside the next), and by the revolving of these spheres (rather than of the earth itself) explained the movement of the heavenly bodies. Hence the servant indirectly compares a man called to high position, but inadequate in it, to a star which does not shine. In the same way, empty sockets "disaster" the checks. "Disaster" refers literally to the calamitous influence of the stars (astrum means star in Latin); here it compares the ruined "cheeks" to the sphere in which no star shines.

Suddenly a trumpet sounds a sennet. (A "sennet" was a group of notes or a tune which was used to identify a particular person, a kind of musical signature). The music introduces the great men and their advisers and captains, Caesar, Antony, Pompey, Lepidus, Agrippa, Maecenas, Enobarbus, Menas, and others. Antony is describing some Egyptian farming customs to Caesar. The farmers can gauge their crops according to the height to which the River Nile rises in flood season. "The higher Nilus swells,/ the more it promises," because the farmers plant their crops in the rich "slime and ooze" left behind when the waters recede. Lepidus pipes up, "You have strange serpents there?" and when Antony answers yes, the tipsy Triumvir ventures a foolish explanation of how Egyptian serpents are bred. "Your serpent of Egypt is bred now of your mud by the operation of your sun: so is your crocodile."

Comment

The belief that living creatures could be generated out of nonliving things (called spontaneous generation) was widely held in Shakespeare's time. The use of the personal pronoun "your" instead of "the" was, then as now, a common colloquialism. Lepidus use of it here, among his betters, is a sign of his drunkenness.

The other leaders take advantage of Lepidus' condition to bait him. Pompey calls for another round of drinks, and offers a toast to him, and though he is sick and would rather not, Lepidus drinks with the rest and goes on talking about Egypt.

While Lepidus is running on about the pyramids, Menas catches Pompey's attention, unnoticed by the others. He wants to speak to his chief alone for a minute, but Pompey, too much enjoying his spoofing of Lepidus, puts him off and pours the groggy general another drink. When Lepidus asks "What manner of thing is your crocodile," Antony takes up the teasing with as nonsensical an explanation of the crocodile as Lepidus had given him of the serpent. "It is shaped, sir, like itself, and it is as broad as it hath breadth: it is just so high as it is, and moves with its own organs. It lives by that which nourisheth it." This seems to satisfy Lepidus, who only asks, "What color is it of?" and learns that it is "of its own color too." "'Tis a strange serpent," he reflects, apparently forgetting that he had asked about crocodiles.

Comment

Antony also says, "the tears of it are wet." This mention of "crocodile tears" alludes to a once-popular belief that after killing a man, and before eating him, the crocodile wept over his body.

Again, Pompey's fun is interrupted by Menas, but this time the pirate's persistence succeeds in separating the host from his guests. The two go apart and, after pledging his loyalty to his chief, Menas asks bluntly, "Wilt thou be lord of all the world?" Pompey thinks he must be mishearing him and has Menas repeat the question. "How should that be," he asks. Menas assures him, "though thou think me poor, I am the man/ Will give you all the world." Now Pompey doubts his friend's sobriety: "Hast thou drunk well?" But Menas denies it: "No, Pompey, I have kept me from the cup"; and assures him again that he can make his chief the master of the world. "Show me which way," Pompey demands, and Menas reveals his scheme. "These three world-sharers, these competitors,/ Are in thy vessel. Let me cut the cable,/ And when we are put off, fall to their throats." Pompey's reaction is surprising. "Ah, this thou shouldst have done" on your own, he says, "and not have spoke on it first." For Menas, his lieutenant, his henchman, it would have been good service to ambush his enemies and kill them; but it would be dishonorable for Pompey himself to allow it. "Being done unknown,/ I should have found it afterwards well done,/ But must condemn it now."

Comment

Pompey's attitude must seem strange. We would expect him either to put political expediency above all and fall in with Menas's murder scheme, or to put his honor and integrity above all and reject the suggestion outright. But Pompey does neither of these - or rather, both. He tries to preserve his personal honor by rejecting any part in the scheme, while at the same time he applauds the treachery behind it and wishes Menas had done it without his knowledge. Surely this is the speech of a moral coward. Pompey wants the profit from the evil deed but not the blame for it. And this lack of courage he labels his "honor."

Menas sees the weakness of Pompey's character through this speech and grows wary of him. He says aside, as if to himself, that he will pull out of his alliance with Pompey because Pompey's good fortune is on the wane; he has the world in his hand and will not take hold of it. "Who seeks and will not take, when once 'tis offer'd," Menas predicts, "Shall never find it more." Pompey turns back to his guests, the genial host once more, to raise another toast to Lepidus. But by this time the tipsy general is under the table.

Comment

Lepidus must have collapsed during the conversation aside between Menas and Pompey, probably when Antony's voice interrupts the scheming of the conspirators to say, "These quick sands, Lepidus,/ Keep off them, for you sink (ll. 59-60)."

So Antony drinks Lepidus' pledge for him and the wine jug goes round again. Pompey fills his cup; Enobarbus toasts Menas and jokes, of the servant who is carrying out the unconscious Lepidus, that he "bears the third part of the world." (Lepidus as a Triumvir rules Africa, approximately one-third of the then known world.) Menas replies that "the third part, then, is drunk: would it were all/ That it might go on wheels!" Again the wine is poured around; again the cups are raised. Pompey complains that the party has not yet reached the frenzy and orgy of an Alexandrian feast at Cleopatra's court. But we're trying, Antony adds, and raises a toast to Caesar to draw him into the drunken revelry.

Comment

"Strike the vessels, ho!" may be Antony's call to the steward to tap the cask of wine, or to the revelers to clash drinking vessels together, as today we might toast by clinking glasses.

Caesar declines another drink at first, but Antony urges him to comply for the sake of the party, and Caesar reluctantly raises his cup to answer Antony's toast. Enobarbus has no such reserve. Already in his cups, he carouses familiarly with Antony, whom he calls "my brave emperor," and suggests they **climax** their celebration with "the Egyptian Bacchanals," a dance in honor of Bacchus, the god of wine in classical mythology.

Pompey is enthusiastic, and Antony bids them all to drink "Till that the conquering wine hath steep'd our sense/ In soft and delicate Lethe." (Lethe was believed by the Greeks to be a river in Hades which caused forgetfulness to those who drank from it.) Enobarbus then officiously places everyone in a ring, joining their hands, and gives instructions for the chorus. The men will carry the burden or **refrain** of the song, while the boy sings the descant. Then the musicians strike up and the drunken leaders reel through their song and dance to an orgiastic **climax** of their "Alexandrian feast." Their song invokes Bacchus, who is both the god of wine and the wine itself they are drinking. They bid him come, with his "pink eyne" (eyes) and his vats of wine, with clusters of grapes to crown their heads and make them all drunk "till the world go round." Hardly have they finished their tipsy song and dance when Caesar breaks off impatiently, chiding his drunken fellows with "What would you more?" He bids a hasty goodnight to Pompey, the host, and begs out with a none too gentle reprimand: "our graver business/ Frowns at this levity." They have all drunk so much, "the wild disguise" (drunkenness) "has almost/ Antick'd us all" (made clowns of us all).

Comment

Caesar's disgust at the drunken cavorting of the others is characteristic of him. Though younger than the rest, he is more proper than they and colder in temperament. He has drunk very little while they have been quaffing freely. We saw earlier how he hesitated to match Antony's toast and only reluctantly drank with him. Now, as the party reels to its highest pitch he can no longer tolerate their drunken excess and decides to call a halt to it. Shakespeare models his character after the Elizabethan ideal of the Roman statesman - shrewd, sober, business-like, but for all that somewhat stiff, intolerant, cold, pompous - a stuffed shirt. So Caesar comes to stand for all the qualities Antony as his opposite, or antagonist, lacks.

At Caesar's urging the party breaks up; the revelers prepare to go ashore. Pompey, however, has no intention of letting the party die, so he offers to "try" Antony once more "on the shore." "And shall, sir" Antony accepts, "give's your hand," and the two erstwhile enemies grow maudlin over their boozy friendship. The stage is empty now but for Menas and Enobarbus, who decline to go ashore to continue the party and stagger off to Menas's cabin instead.

SUMMARY

This famous scene of the drinking bout aboard Pompey's galley seems intended exclusively to develop character and create atmosphere. Four of the characters drink too much:

1. Lepidus, the weakest of the Triumvirs heretofore, shows himself again to be inconsequential, a fool, the butt of the others' jokes.

2. Enobarbus drinks and makes merry with the same openness and gusto that he shows at other times.

3. Pompey plays the genial host, but under the geniality he reveals a nature that is morally weak and altogether too trusting and optimistic.

4. Although it is Pompey's party, Antony winds up leading it and turning it into an "Egyptian Bacchanal," so that much of the excess in the scene must be associated with him. Two are more temperate in their drinking:

5. Menas, the unscrupulous pirate, keeps his wits about him so as to take advantage of those who are drowning theirs. His scheme to subvert the Triumvirs is an exemplary piece of Machiavellian treachery which violates every sacred bond of trust and hospitality.

6. Caesar abstains for its own sake, because in excessive drinking he will lose the clarity and self-control which he feels proper to his position. He takes himself very seriously and fears to be made a fool or to make a fool of himself. The scene is a Roman imitation of an Alexandrian feast: the inebriety and excess of Egypt have infected sober Italy. Though we may be put off by his aloofness, we must be impressed by Caesar's sobriety and sense of responsibility. And we can foresee already that Caesar, though a lesser man and soldier than Antony, is destined to triumph over him.

ANTONY AND CLEOPATRA

TEXTUAL ANALYSIS

ACT 3: SCENES 1 - 6

ACT 3, SCENE 1

This scene takes us to Syria where Ventidius, Antony's lieutenant, has accomplished his mission and defeated the Parthian hordes who had swept across the frontiers of the eastern provinces of the Roman Empire.

Comment

When we recall that there were originally no act divisions in this play we see that it is not by chance that this scene comes next. In fact, Shakespeare achieves a striking dramatic effect by taking us immediately from the drunken debauchery of Pompey's galley to Ventidius's military triumph on the plain of Syria. For it is the underling, Ventidius, who alone maintains his nobility by fighting Rome's legitimate enemies, not his fellow Romans. And even he must be cautious, lest he antagonize Antony.

Ventidius enters in triumphal procession behind the slaughtered body of his enemy, Pacorus, the Parthian general. He claims that his victory over "darting Parthia" and the death of Pacorus revenge the defeat and death of Marcus Crassus.

> Comment

Together with Pompey the Great and Julius Caesar, Marcus Crassus formed the first Triumvirate. He was defeated by the Parthians in 53 B.C. and was treacherously killed by Orodes (father of Pacorus and king of Parthia) during a council of truce. His unavenged murder was a cause of popular complaint in Rome.

When Silius urges Ventidius to follow up his victory by pursuing the routed Parthians through Media and Mesopotamia, Ventidius is cautious. "I have done enough," he says. Rather than praise and honor, he would win Antony's displeasure for his pains. "For learn this, Silius;/ Better to leave undone, than by our deed/ Acquire too high a fame, when him we serve's away." He is afraid that if he makes too good a showing, defeats the enemy too soundly, Antony will be jealous of his renown. He quotes the example of Sossius, like himself one of Antony's lieutenants, in Syria, whose victories gained him renown and lost his captain's favor. "Who does i' the wars more than his captain can,/ Becomes his captain's captain ..." (There is no authority in Plutarch for the story of Sossius's dismissal.) Paradoxically, the soldier's ambition is better served by gaining less than he might, than by gaining more. "I could do more to do Antonius good,/ But 'twould offend him. And in his offence/ Should my performance perish." Silius acknowledges the wisdom of Ventidius' words; without such wisdom a soldier is no better than his sword. Then Ventidius' tells how he will inform Antony of his victory, making it seem Antony's victory, disclaiming any credit for himself. Silius asks where their captain is now, and we learn from Ventidius' reply that Antony is on his way to Athens and that they plan to meet him there. With that the victorious lieutenant disappears from the play.

SUMMARY

This scene accomplishes the following:

1. Concludes the subplot of the Parthian invasion.

2. Develops the character of Ventidius further in order to contrast him with the other generals.

ACT 3, SCENE 2

Ventidius' mention of Antony's going to Athens is the cue for this shift back to Rome. Here we shall see the newly-married Antony and Octavia taking leave of Caesar and Lepidus. Shakespeare introduces their farewells with the farewell conversation between the outspoken Enobarbus (leaving with Antony) and the politic Agrippa, which comments on the scene about to take place. We learn from their exchange that the "brothers" - an ironic description of the new accord between Pompey, Caesar, Antony, Lepidus-are parting. Pompey is already gone (back to Sicily and Antony) is preparing to leave for Athens. "Octavia weeps/ To part from Rome;" Enobarbus says, and "Caesar is sad." However, they direct most of their sarcasm at Lepidus, who "since Pompey's feast ... is troubled with the green-sickness." (Green-sickness was a kind of anemia believed to affect love-sick young girls. Here it may be used sarcastically to describe Lepidus who is "in love" with Caesar and Antony.) They mimic Lepidus' fawning adulation of his two partners: "O, how he loves Caesar!" But how dearly he adores Mark Antony!" If Caesar is "the Jupiter of men," then Antony is "the god of Jupiter." (Jupiter was father of the gods; high praise indeed to be god of Jupiter.) If Caesar is "the nonpareil" or utterly incomparable, then Antony is the "Arabian bird!" (The phoenix bird, a fabled creature, only one of which existed at any time.) And so on. Lepidus plies "them both with excellent praises," yet can praise neither enough. "Hoo! hearts, tongues, figures, scribes, bards, poets, cannot/ Think, speak, cast, write, sing, number, hoo,/ His love to Antony," Enobarbus parodies the sonneteers.

Comment

This device-a compound subject paralleled by a compound verb, each of the latter appropriate to one of the former-was characteristic of some Elizabethan sonneteers. Since sonnets were often love-poems of extravagant praise, Enobarbus indirectly compares the infatuated Lepidus with one of these love-sick sonneteers.

Their fun is interrupted by a signal for Enobarbus to mount, and they exchange farewells.

Comment

Although the cues are unmistakable, the two evidently do not part and leave the stage here because they are present during the rest of the scene and make comments upon it (see 2. 51 ff.).

Perhaps they are about to leave but are detained by the entrance of Caesar, Antony, Lepidus, and Octavia. These four have come, like Enobarbus and Agrippa, to say goodbye. But the light note of wit and banter changes now to one of sadness as brother and sister take their leave. Caesar gives each a final admonition: to his sister to "prove such a wife as my thoughts make thee"; to Antony to "let not the piece of virtue which is set/ Betwixt us, as the cement of our love/ To keep it builded, be the ram to batter/ The fortress of it …"

Comment

Of course, this is just what Enobarbus predicted earlier (Act 2, Scene 6), and what will actually occur later (Act 3, Scene 6).

Antony's back goes up at this advice, and he protests that Caesar has no grounds for such a fear. When Caesar turns to Octavia for a last goodbye, the tears start from his sister's eyes. She is so broken up emotionally, "her tongue will not obey her heart, nor can/ Her heart inform her tongue," and she must whisper her goodbyes in Caesar's ear.

Comment

Antony compares her to "the swan's down feather/ That stands upon the swell at the full tide,/ And neither way inclines." Torn between brother and husband, like a feather between tides, she can go neither way.

Here Enobarbus is so surprised by any show of tender emotion in Caesar that he questions Agrippa aside, "Will Caesar weep?" (Obviously they have not left the stage; furthermore, their presence is unknown to the others.) Agrippa believes he may, because "He has a cloud in his face." Enobarbus replies that a cloud in the face is a bad sign in a horse and in a man as well.

> Comment

Agrippa uses the cloud as a **metaphor**: as a cloud brings rain, so the sadness in Caesar's face will bring tears. Enobarbus uses a different **metaphor**. A "cloud" in a horse's face refers to some marking (perhaps the absence of a white star) regarded as a blemish. So Enobarbus regards tears or any soft emotion as a blemish in a man, and particularly in Caesar.

Agrippa disagrees and accuses Antony of similar softness. (Enobarbus is almost taunting Agrippa with Caesar's tender youth; Agrippa cites Antony because he is old and battle-hardened.) Did he not weep when he found Julius Caesar dead, and when he found Brutus slain after Philippi? But Enobarbus cynically dismisses Antony's tears as hypocritical-so much water, "a rheum." He wept over sorrow that he himself had caused; he wept until even the cynical Enobarbus wept with him. The two interlopers retire again to the background; Antony and Caesar embrace; Octavia bestows a final parting kiss on her brother and, trumpets sounding, the newlyweds start on their journey.

SUMMARY

> The main purpose of this scene is to dramatize the close bond of affection between Caesar and his sister, so that this love may motivate him later in the play. We also see in what contempt Lepidus is held for fawning over his betters to keep in their good graces.

ACT 3, SCENE 3

Back in Alexandria we find Cleopatra where we left her in Act 2, Scene 5, although considerable time has elapsed. Recovered from her original shock and despair at Antony's marriage, she summons the messenger again before her to learn more about Antony's new wife. Naturally he is terrified and reluctant to appear, but the queen is in good humor and soon puts him sufficiently at his ease. When she is sure he has actually seen Octavia with his own eyes, she pumps him for information about her appearance. "Is she as tall as me?" she asks, and learns she is not. "Didst hear her speak?" she asks; "Is she shrill-tongu'd or low?" "She is low-voic'd," the boy replies, and Cleopatra reflects, "That's not so good: he cannot like her long."

Comment

There are two interpretations of this line. Cleopatra thinks:

1. A low voice is unpleasant: therefore Antony cannot like Octavia long.

2. That piece of news about Octavia is not so good (so far as Cleopatra is concerned): Nevertheless, Antony cannot like her long. The first is supported by what comes immediately after (1. 16) and by the absence of a conjunction after the colon: we would usually read it as "therefore."

The second is supported by the meanings of the words themselves. Octavia's low voice would certainly be more attractive to Antony than a shrill one (compare Act 1, Scene 1, Line 32). Hence this piece of news is discouraging to Cleopatra.

Charmian is quick to agree with her queen, and that little bit of encouragement is all she needs. Cleopatra wants desperately to believe the worst reports about her rival, so wishful thinking soon turns all Octavia's felicities to faults. Her soothing voice and petiteness become "dull of tongue, and dwarfish." Heartened by her "discovery," Cleopatra moves onto surer ground with "What majesty is in her gait?" and adds the naked threat, "Remember if e'er thou look'dst on majesty." The messenger takes the hint, falls in with Cleopatra's self-deception. "She creeps," he answers, and from now on his enthusiasm for the game will feed hers. "He's very knowing," she says, "The fellow has good judgment," because he has told her what she wants to hear. So when she asks him how old Octavia is, he starts by saying, "She was a widow," because that will soften the fact that she is considerably younger than the aging Cleopatra. When he admits that Octavia is thirty, Cleopatra does not even acknowledge it but rushes on to question him about Octavia's looks. Is her face long or round, she asks, and of course he replies, "Round, even to faultiness." Not only is she moon-faced, which signifies foolishness, but her forehead is extremely low as well.

Comment

In Shakespeare's time a low forehead was considered a mark of ugliness. Physiognomy (a pseudo-science which claimed to evaluate character from the facial features) taught that a round head and face denoted a foolish person. Compare the picture of Octavia which emerges from this interview with that drawn by Agrippa earlier, in Act 2, Scene 2, which is based on Plutarch, and with what Octavia shows of herself in the play. The noblewoman-sister and wife to emperors-whose virtue, graces, and beauty make her a match for "the best of men"; and who demonstrates her honesty and loyalty toward both husband and brother later in the play (Act 3, Scene 4 and Scene 6); is travestied in Cleopatra's jealous eyes as dwarfish, dull of tongue, creepy, lifeless, aging, with a round face that bespeaks a foolish wit, and with a treacherously low forehead. Love's self-delusions are made to appear very amusing in this scene.

Charmian, out of pity for her queen and happy to see her happy, continues to flatter Cleopatra's mood, after the messenger leaves with a handful of gold for having been so obliging. She agrees that Octavia is nothing to lose sleep over and that the messenger's report is to be trusted. "The man hath seen some majesty," Cleopatra vaunts of herself, "and should know." Charmian agrees, a little too effusively, and leads her mistress off to write letters to Antony.

SUMMARY

Still nothing new in Alexandria to further the story. Shakespeare fills out his portrait of Cleopatra in yet another of her moods.

ACT 3, SCENES 4 & 5

Antony and Octavia have arrived in Athens. Already the rift between the two Emperors has begun to widen, and Octavia finds herself left in the breach. The scene opens in the middle of their conversation. Evidently Octavia has been defending her brother against Antony's charges, but has been fighting a losing battle. Now he raises his bitterest complaint. Caesar (1) has waged new wars against Pompey in violation of their agreement; (2) has made his will and read it; (3) has attacked Antony's honor and reputation indirectly by speaking grudgingly of him.

> Comment

The second complaint is pointless on the face of it. What offense would Caesar give Antony by publishing his own will? But Plutarch tells us that it was Antony's will that Caesar got hold of by force and read aloud to the Senators to discredit his partner. Since it is unlikely that Shakespeare would depart from his source on so crucial a point, we must assume a corruption in the text.

Octavia defends her brother by claiming that perhaps these reports are not all true, or if true, perhaps not as offensive as they sound. She laments her position in the quarrel, abandoned between the two, her love and prayers equally divided. Antony woos her to his side of the quarrel, telling her that if Caesar succeeds in destroying his reputation she would as well be not married at all as married to him. He will be like a great tree left branchless. But he urges her to mediate between them as she has requested, and informs her that in the meantime he is raising an army which will eclipse her brother's. Scene 5 also takes place in Antony's house in Athens. When these two leave, Enobarbus and Eros come on to gossip about the latest news. They disclose that Caesar, after joining with Lepidus to defeat Pompey, turned on his erstwhile partner and denied him an equal share of the victory. Besides this, under the pretext of some "treasonous" letters which Lepidus had formerly written to Pompey, and with no other proof than his own accusation, he threw his former partner into jail to await execution.

> Comment

We see now what Shakespeare's characterization of Lepidus has been moving towards. Having made the Emperor of Africa weak, inconsequential, and unstable, Shakespeare has no trouble getting rid of him, almost, as it were, behind the scenes.

Enobarbus responds to Eros's news with a flippant **metaphor** that pictures the world as so much food, ground between "a pair of chaps," i.e., the upper and lower jaws (Antony and Caesar). Antony has heard the news also and is upset by it, Eros reports. He is also outraged that one of his own officers has murdered Pompey.

Comment

After Pompey was defeated in Sicily by Caesar and Lepidus, he fled to the East, plotting against Antony's provinces. When his designs failed he was killed by Titius, one of Antony's officers, and probably at Antony's command. Here Antony is shown to reject any responsibility for it.

The backstairs gossip continues. We are informed that a great fleet has been equipped, ready to sail against Caesar. Eros finally gets around to the point of his errand: Antony wishes to speak with Enobarbus. Enobarbus shrugs the message off: the meeting will be pointless. Then he asks Eros to lead him to Antony, and the two go off.

SUMMARY

These two scenes mainly serve to bring us up to date on what has been happening among the Triumvirate. We learn that:

1. Antony and Caesar have had a falling out and Octavia has gone back to Rome to try to patch it up.

2. Caesar and Lepidus have attacked and defeated Pompey, despite their treaty of peace.

3. Pompey is dead, murdered in the East by one of Antony's lieutenants.

4. Caesar has jailed Lepidus on trumped-up charges and plans to execute him.

5. Antony has readied a great fleet to sail against Caesar at any moment.

ACT 3, SCENE 6

As Scene 4 opened in the middle of Antony's denunciation of Caesar, this scene, back in Rome, finds Caesar denouncing Antony before his two advisers, Agrippa and Maecenas. He immediately reveals a new development in the story: Antony has left Athens a while before and has gone to Alexandria-to his mistress there.

Comment

Antony must have left Athens shortly after Octavia did. His compliance in her journey to Rome can now be seen in its proper light.

In Alexandria Antony has resumed his former life in the Egyptian court and has cast further insults on Rome. Caesar enumerates them: (1) He has had, or allowed, himself and his mistress to be publicly enthroned amidst extravagant display in the market-place. (2) He has given public recognition and a place of honor to Caesarius, Cleopatra's son by Julius Caesar, and all of their own "unlawful" offspring. (3) He has conferred independence on Egypt and made Cleopatra absolute queen over it and several other conquered territories: Lower Syria, Cyprus, and Lydia (Shakespeare follows North's confusion here, giving Lydia for Plutarch's Libya, but corrects himself later, when North does, in line 69, "Bocchus, the king of Libya"). (4) He has proclaimed his sons kings of kings. (5) He has given outright the conquered territories of Media, Parthia and Armenia to his son Alexander. (6) To his son Ptolemy he has assigned Syria, Cilicia and Phoenicia. (7) His mistress, Cleopatra, appeared that day, and often in audiences, dressed as the goddess Isis (chief Egyptian goddess; patroness of motherhood and fertility).

Comment

This condemnation of Antony is, of course, from the viewpoint of Imperial Rome. It is taken with few substantive changes from Plutarch and reflects his sympathy for the Roman position which strongly opposed the creation of independent kingdoms within territories conquered by the Empire. He calls Antony's division of lands "arrogant and insolent... and done in derision and contempt of the Romanes."

Caesar's advisers urge him to make these complaints public, so as to turn popular opinion, which is already "queasy," completely against Antony.

Comment

The people are disgusted with Antony, North says, because of his treatment of Octavia. "For her honest love and regard to her husband made every man hate him, when they saw he did so unkindly use so noble a lady..."

"The people know it" already, Caesar replies, and have even heard Antony's accusations in turn. They are: (1) That Caesar took Sicily from Pompey but did not cut him in on the spoils. (2) That he loaned Caesar some ships and never got them back. (3) That Caesar despised Lepidus, then never split his confiscated property with Antony. And Caesar in turn has answered Antony's accusations. He has told him: (1) That Lepidus was put down because he had grown too cruel and abused his high position. (2) That he is perfectly willing to give Antony a share of all the spoils he has conquered, but in return demands a share of Armenia and all the other kingdoms Antony has conquered on his own.

> Comment

Shakespeare repeats North's account that Lepidus "did overcruelly use his authoritie." But this does not at all agree with his characterization as mild and ineffectual, which Shakespeare has given Lepidus up till now.

They realize, of course, that Antony will never agree to the conditions. Suddenly, unexpectedly, Octavia walks in on the three conversing men. Caesar is first of all shocked to see her back in Rome, then pleased, then angry. He is shocked because he had no inkling she was not still in Athens, even though Antony had left for Egypt. He is pleased to see her because of the great affection he bears for his sister: "That ever I should call thee castaway!" he gently chides her. He is angry that she should arrive so quietly, so unannounced, almost so stealthily. She, Caesar's sister, wife of Antony, "should have an army for an usher," and their marching feet should have beaten a cloud of dust "to the roof of heaven" to tell of her approach. But she has come, he chides, like "a market-maid to Rome," and in coming so quietly has prevented a mammoth welcome and demonstration of love on their part. They would have given her the red-carpet treatment.

Comment

Naturally there is an implied criticism of Antony's niggardliness, if not an open suggestion of it in the mention of his name. Caesar is hurt on two accounts: (1) that Antony has neglected to provide properly for his wife's journey; (2) that he himself has not been allowed to provide properly for her welcome. Apart from its place in the story and characterization, this speech of Caesar's has another function in the play. There is an obvious contrast between Octavia's arrival in Rome and Cleopatra's arrival in Tarsus, as narrated by Enobarbus in Act 2, Scene 2.

But Octavia dismisses his objections and defends her husband. She was not forced to travel thus unaccompanied, but chose to do so for swiftness' sake. Antony agreed to her journey when he heard of Caesar's war preparations. Rather to get rid of you, Caesar answers, because you stood "'tween his lust and him."

Comment

There are two interpretations of the line, "Which soon he granted/ Being an abstract 'tween his lust and him." One reads this as "obstruct," meaning "you (Octavia) stood between Antony and Cleopatra"; the other holds the original "abstract" refers not to Octavia, but to her absence which allows Antony to have his desire.

"Where is he now?" he tests her. And when she replies "in Athens," he breaks the news ungently to her, "No, my most wronged sister, Cleopatra/ Hath nodded him to her." "He hath given his empire/ Up to a whore," he says, and then goes on to rehearse the list of kings and kingdoms that Antony has marshaled for his war against Rome (Shakespeare's list follows closely that of North). Octavia's heart is broken by this threatened break between the emperors, for she loves both men. Caesar tries to win her to his side. He has held back from openly attacking Antony thus far, he says, until he could be sure of two things: (1) that Antony in any way abused or mistreated Octavia; (2) that his own empire was in danger of attack. Now that he has evidence of both, the break must come. But, he says, think of this war as justice, who "makes his ministers of us, and those that love you." Again he welcomes her warmly to Rome; Agrippa and Maecena join him in extending their welcome, and the scene closes for the last time on a bewildered and broken-hearted Octavia.

SUMMARY

Much is accomplished in this scene. We learn:

1. Antony has enthroned himself and Cleopatra in the public market-place in Alexandria.

2. He has created an independent Egypt and made Cleopatra its absolute queen.

3. He has parceled out other conquered territories to Cleopatra's sons.

4. He has enlisted a number of eastern kingdoms in a war against Caesar.

5. Caesar, to avenge Octavia's honor and defend his own empire, is prepared to attack Egypt and Antony.

ANTONY AND CLEOPATRA

TEXTUAL ANALYSIS

ACT 3: SCENES 7 - 13

ACT 3, SCENE 7

This scene is set in Antony's camp near Actium (on the west coast of Greece, across the Ionian Sea from the heel of the Italian boot). Enobarbus is arguing with Cleopatra that she should not take a personal part in the battle that is brewing. She claims that since the war was declared against her, she should be there in person. Enobarbus answers with a **metaphor** under his breath. If they were to use both stallions and mares in battle, the stallions would be so distracted by the mares that their services would be lost altogether: "the mares would bear/ A Soldier and his horse." Cleopatra does not hear what he says, so he explains his objection aloud. Her presence, he says, will only distract Antony's attention from the battle and prevent him from doing his best. They cannot afford that now. Already in Rome they are laughed at because it is joked "that Photinus, an eunuch [Mardian] and [Cleopatra's] maids/ Manage this war." But Cleopatra disdains Rome and its rumors. She has contributed heavily to Antony's forces and she will be present at the battle as head of her kingdom. Enobarbus breaks off the argument as Antony enters with Canidius, one of his captains. They are discussing Caesar's rapid maneuver, by which he has already transported his armies from the southwest coast of Italy across the Ionian Sea, to take Antony by surprise at Actium. Antony decides to meet his enemy by sea. Cleopatra agrees, "By sea, what else?" but Canidius asks him why. And Antony's only answer is because "he dares us to't." So you have dared him to single combat, Enobarbus objects, "Ay, and to wage this battle at Pharsalia ..." Canidius seconds him; but Caesar has shrugged off both dares because neither is to his advantage. "And so should you," Canidius advises. Enobarbus argues against a naval encounter for several reasons: (1) Antony's fleet is less experienced than Caesar's. Caesar's navy fought against Pompey; Antony's ships are manned by landlubbers-captured mule drivers and farmers-pressed into service quickly to fill the need. (2) Caesar's ships are light and maneuverable, built for warfare; Antony's, mainly borrowed, are heavy and built for display. (3) Antony holds the absolute advantage over Caesar's land army, in numbers and experience, and is himself the master strategist. He sacrifices his advantages and lays himself open to chance and hazard by choosing a sea battle. Still, Antony is firm: "I'll fight by sea." And we know the real reason for his firmness when Cleopatra joins in: "I have sixty sails, Caesar none better." So, committed to a sea encounter he is ill-prepared for, Antony draws up his strategy. He will burn all the ships he cannot fully man and meet Caesar's invasion head on as it approaches the headland of Actium from Toryne. "But if we fail," he second-guesses himself, "When then can do't at land," hoping to destroy the enemy forces on the beaches. When a messenger arrives to confirm the presence of Caesar's army at Toryne, the battle is joined. Antony is dumbfounded by Caesar's swiftness, but issues orders for Canidius to command his nineteen legions and twelve thousand cavalry on the beaches while he takes to his flagship to command the fleet. But before he can leave, an old soldier comes before him to raise his seasoned voice to beg Antony to avoid a naval engagement. "Trust not to rotten planks," he begs, but all he gets for his pains is Antony's brusque "Well, well, away!" He is eager for his do m. Now the stage is left to the old soldier, who spills out his anguish to the more receptive ears of Canidius. "So our leader's led," the latter agrees, "And we are women's men," referring to Cleopatra's power over Antony. But at least they have salvaged a sizable land contingent; all may not be lost. The two soldiers exchange news; Canidius learns that Caesar's lieutenant is an old acquaintance of his, Taurus. And then their gossip is interrupted by a messenger who summons Canidius to Antony.

SUMMARY

This scene is crucial to the outcome of the play. It explains these important developments:

1. The swiftness of Caesar's naval attack and Antony's lack of preparation to meet it successfully.

2. Cleopatra's presence in the heat of the forthcoming battle (very important) and her poor advice in urging a naval encounter.

3. The unanimous opposition of Antony's soldiers to the battle, and their advice to fight on land.

4. Caesar's arrival and capture of Toryne, from whence he attacks Actium.

ACT 3, SCENES 8-10

These three brief scenes keep us informed of the battle's progress. In Scene 8 Caesar gives orders to his lieutenant, Taurus, leading his troops. Caesar tells him not to attack Antony on land until after the naval battle is over, and hands him a scroll containing further orders and battle plans. Scene 9 shows the same thing happening on the other side. Antony gives Enobarbus instructions where to station his troops for the coming battle so they can watch the developments at sea (and, incidentally, so that Enobarbus and Scarus will have a good vantage from which to describe the battle in the next scene). Scene 10 is the actual battle scene, but of course we do not see it directly. First, Canidius marches across the stage with a group of Antony's soldiers, then Taurus does the same with some of Caesar's, and when they are gone, the noise of a sea fight is heard off-stage. Suddenly Enobarbus rushes on stage to spread the alarm. Cleopatra's flagship, The Antoniad, has turned and run from the battle! And behind her, following in full retreat, fly all sixty of the Egyptian ships. He cannot believe his eyes. But there is no mistake about it. On rushes Scarus to verify the defeat. "We have kiss'd away/ Kingdoms, and provinces," he cries in despair. How does the battle look now, Enobarbus asks, and Scarus answers, "On our side, like the token'd pestilence,/ Where death is sure."

Comment

"The token'd pestilence" refers to a symptom of the plague. When red spots appeared on the victim it was a sure sign he would soon be dead. These spots were called "God's tokens."

Antony's defeat is sure, because when his ships were beginning to get the upper hand, that worn-out jade, Cleopatra, like a cow stung by a gad-fly in the heat of summer, hoisted a full sail to the wind and scurried off in fright. This Enobarbus already knows; but there is worse still to come. For, seeing his mistress' ships in flight, Antony hoisted his sails and took off after her, leaving the battle at its very height, and still undecided. "I never saw action of such shame," Scarus adds.

Comment

Both Romans take this as an evil sign of Cleopatra's magic power over Antony, who now has violated even his code as a soldier.

Canidius enters, full of the tragic news, and complains bitterly that the defeat is all Antony's fault. He echoes Scarus's opinion that Antony is not himself, hinting that Cleopatra holds some magic power over him. And Canidius adds, "O! he has given example for our flight ..." He intends to surrender his legions of soldiers and cavalry to Caesar. Already six other kings have done the same and fled to the Peloponnesus. Scarus has half a mind to join him; but he decides to wait and see what will happen. Enobarbus decides against his better judgment to stick by Antony.

SUMMARY

These three scenes describing the battle produce three important developments:

1. Antony loses the naval encounter with Caesar because Cleopatra ups sail and runs, for no reason, and he follows behind her.

2. Antony's comrades no longer trust his leadership. They believe he is under Cleopatra's evil influence, and have begun to go over to the enemy side.

3. Canidius decides to turn against Antony; Scarus wants to, but decides to wait; Enobarbus, against his better judgment, still sticks by his foundering lord.

ACT 3, SCENE 11

Some days have passed since the defeat at Actium. We find Antony back in Cleopatra's palace in Alexandria. He is off by himself, moody and crest-fallen over his cowardly performance. Only a few attendants are with him, and even them he urges to "fly,/ And make your peace with Caesar."

He is terribly ashamed and depressed over his recent defeat; he feels his cowardly example has instructed others to do likewise. "To run, and show their shoulders" - referring to those kings who have gone over to the enemy. Evidently contemplating suicide in his despair, he urges his friends to follow the others to Caesar's ranks. He offers them gold and letters of introduction to smooth their path and make their betrayal easier. Only, he prays, "look not sad,/ Nor make replies of loathness." He begs, not commands, them to leave him to himself, for he feels he has lost all right to command. Just as he slumps to his seat in utter dejection, Cleopatra is led on by her attendants Charmian and Iras, and Antony's lieutenant, Eros. Eros has evidently brought her to try to comfort his lord. The others second his urgings. But despite them, the two estranged lovers remain aloof at first. Antony reflects aloud how Caesar at Philippi wore his sword merely for show, "like a dancer," while he did the actual fighting.

"Yet now ... ?" he adds wistfully. Moved by this speech and by the entreaties of her attendants, Cleopatra relents and goes to comfort him. "O, whither hast thou led me Egypt?" he addresses her, and confesses that he has been avoiding her out of shame. But she blames herself. "Forgive my fearful sails!" she begs, "I little thought/ You would have followed." You knew I would, he replies, for I was bound to you by my heart strings. You knew you had me completely in your power. Then he complains that he is reduced to groveling before the youthful Caesar, begging favors-he who once ruled half the world. All because he loves her. "Pardon, pardon!" Cleopatra cries through her tears, overcome by sorrow. Instantly the scolding soldier is dissolved and goes to comfort his comforter. "Fall not a tear" he soothes her, for "one of them rates [is worth]/ All that is won and lost." When she is quiet again, he asks if "our schoolmaster" has come back.

Comment

North tells us that "our schoolmaster" is Euphronius, the tutor to Antony's children by Cleopatra. We will learn in the next scene that Antony has sent him as an ambassador to beg terms of surrender from Caesar. That he should entrust such important affairs to so lowly a messenger is a sign of how far his fortunes have fallen.

Then Antony calls for wine to lift their spirits and cries his defiance to fortune as the scene ends.

SUMMARY

This scene explains Antony's defeat at Actium and prepares us for his final defeat later. It shows:

1. That Antony, for the first time, realizes how completely he is overpowered by his love for Cleopatra and how this has caused him humiliation and defeat.

2. That Cleopatra recognizes her guilt in that defeat, but claims she intended no treachery by it.

3. How the lovers are reconciled because Antony is powerless to remove himself from Cleopatra's influence.

ACT 3, SCENE 12

Antony mentioned "our schoolmaster" at the end of the last scene; now his reference is explained. At Caesar's camp in Egypt the schoolmaster (Euphronius) comes before Caesar and his advisors-Agrippa, Dolabella, Thidias, and others-as Antony's ambassador to ask for terms of surrender. Dolabella takes it as a sign of Antony's weakness, who before could make his conquered kings errand boys, to send a lowly schoolteacher. The ambassador delivers his message. Antony surrenders and acknowledges Caesar as his lord in exchange for two requests: (1) That he may remain in Egypt, or if that is too much to ask, that he be allowed to live out his days as a private citizen in Athens. (2) That Cleopatra may keep the crown of Egypt for her heirs while recognizing Caesar's supremacy. Caesar turns down Antony's request outright. As for Cleopatra, he tells the messenger, she can have whatever favor she chooses on one condition: that she drive Antony out of Egypt or kill him there. The schoolmaster bows himself out to deliver his message. Then Caesar calls Thidias before him, to entrust him with an important mission.

Comment

Shakespeare follows North's account of Thidias' embassy to Cleopatra, but unaccountably changes the ambassador's name in doing so from Thyreus (North's version) to Thidias.

He dispatches this smooth diplomat to seduce Cleopatra away from Antony by eloquence and flattery and extravagant promises. He hopes that her marred fortunes with Antony will make her more receptive to a new lover. Caesar cautions Thidias also to observe how Antony's spirit is bearing up under his misfortunes and disgrace.

SUMMARY

A short scene, this nevertheless provides us with important information about the development of the plot:

1. Caesar denies Antony's request for asylum; he plans a fight to the finish, "give no quarter, take no quarter."

2. Caesar hopes to divide his enemy in order to conquer, by winning Cleopatra away from her disgraced lover.

ACT 3, SCENE 13

Gloom is thick in the halls of Cleopatra's palace. Through it Cleopatra, Enobarbus, Charmian and Iras try to see some brightness in the future. "What shall we do," the queen questions Enobarbus, and he answers bleakly, "Think, and die." But he reassures the queen that she is not to blame for the defeat at Actium; Antony is man enough and soldier enough, or should be, not to let "the itch of his affection" spoil his judgment in battle. He should have known better than to follow her ships in flight. It is the old conflict in Antony between reason and passion. Cleopatra silences him suddenly as Antony enters, speaking loudly with his returned ambassador, Euphronius. He repeats Caesar's offer to Cleopatra: her kingdom for Antony's head. With four words she shows it is unthinkable: "That head, my lord?"

> Comment

How much more love this simple and indirect question carries than any loud refusal or protestation!

So Antony sends the ambassador back with his refusal and a challenge to cap it. He accuses Caesar of cowardice and ineptitude: His captains win his battles for him. And he dares his brother-in-law to a duel, single combat, "sword against sword," as he leads the schoolteacher off to write it out in a letter.

> Comment

Unlike the offer of surrender earlier, this message must bear the authority and seal of the sender because of the explosive nature of its contents.

Enobarbus shakes his head at this. Antony has lost his sense along with his sovereignty if he seriously believes Caesar will accept such a ridiculous challenge. Would ever the winner, riding high, give up his advantage and descend to fight on foot with the loser? "Caesar," he exclaims aside, "thou hast subdued/ His judgment too," A servant enters to announce a messenger from Caesar (the messenger is Thidias, dispatched by Caesar at the end of Scene 12). Cleopatra notices that he does not show any of the deference or forms of courtesy which servants are accustomed to use when they address their queen.

Comment

There are several such touches in this scene with which Shakespeare shows that Antony and Cleopatra, because of their disgrace, have lost prestige and authority among their own people, kings and menials alike. Notice the **irony** of her final words: "Admit him, sir." She addresses the servant as if he were better than he really is because he has pretended to be.

The servant's impertinence causes Enobarbus to consider again whether he should get out while there is still time. If we are loyal to a fool, he reflects, our loyalty is mere folly. But the man who can endure "To follow with allegiance a fall'n lord," conquers his conqueror "and earns a place i' the story."

Comment

There are two possible interpretations of these lines, depending upon the meaning of "To follow with allegiance a fall'n lord." (1) If it means merely to stick by him in defeat, then Enobarbus is saying that such selfless loyalty will win the admiration of the conqueror and secure a place of honor for the loyal soldier. (2) But it may mean to follow one's lord even to death, the normal course of suicide for the defeated in Roman times. So we speak of a soldier "fallen in battle." If the loyal soldier follows his lord even to death, he escapes the ignominy and disgrace of being captured, "and earns a place in the story." It is Antony's other lieutenant, Eros, who proves this loyalty unto death; and it is his name we remember affectionately at the end of this story.

Thidias enters on his errand of seduction. At first, Cleopatra is brusque with him. Naturally he wants to speak to her alone; but she will not dismiss her friends. So he starts by mentioning Caesar's generosity and leniency. Immediately he gives Cleopatra a ready-made excuse by saying that Caesar realizes she did not choose to consort with Antony out of love, but out of fear. Therefore, Caesar pities her frailties rather than blames them. Cleopatra falls in with the scheme. She accepts Caesar's out and denies she ever yielded her honor willingly. She was conquered by Antony. Enobarbus, overhearing their exchange is disgusted by her disloyalty, for he believes Cleopatra is turning against Antony and accepting Caesar's overtures of friendship. Outraged, he storms out to look for Antony and warn him of Cleopatra's treachery. He reflects again that Antony is like a sinking ship; even his dearest friends abandon him. With Enobarbus gone, Thidias presses his advantage. Caesar is generous as well as forgiving. If Cleopatra will quit Antony and put herself under Caesar's protection, she may have whatever she desires from him. To show her willingness, she grasps Thidias' hand and kisses it, in proxy for Caesar's feet to hear his judgment. Thidias commends her wisdom and nobility in choosing Caesar above Antony and bends to kiss her hand. As he does so, Enobarbus rushes back in with Antony just in time to witness what seems to both the emblem of her perfidy and the besmirching of her honor. Antony is furious: The storm breaks.

Comment

It is important that we are not taken in by Cleopatra's act as Thidias and Enobarbus and Antony are. We must never doubt Cleopatra's love and loyalty to Antony for an instant: we shall have ample proof of both at the end.

But Antony has seen just enough to convince him of the opposite. He berates Thidias severely as a "kite," but does not yell at Cleopatra in public, while any underlings are in the room. Then he sends Caesar's personal emissary out to be whipped like a common hoodlum because he dared to grow too familiar with Cleopatra's hand.

Comment

The term "Jack" was used contemptuously to mean a common rascal. It was such a common name in England that it came to be used in a number of epithets: "Jack the Journeyman"; "Jacks of all trades"; "Jack in office"; "Jack," or "knave," of "hearts" (playing cards), etc.

When the servants have dragged Thidias off, Antony turns on Cleopatra. He reflects bitterly on all that he has given up for her sake: his place in Rome; his wife Octavia, a "gem of women"; and the lawful children she would have borne him. And for what? To be made ridiculous by a queen who flirts with her servants! He shouts over her protests; he accuses her of always having been shifty and calculating, but says his better judgment has been so blinded by his passion that he has adored her for the very tricks and wiles by which she has deceived him. His anger rages like a fire: what he says, instead of damping it, feeds it. He dredges up old grievances against her: he picked her up after she had been dirtied and dropped by others. "I found you as a morsel, cold upon/ Dead Caesar's trencher: nay, you were a fragment/ Of Gnaeus Pompey's ..." (Remember Cleopatra boasted of her youthful conquests in Act I, Scene 5). She does not know the meaning of chastity, he says. While she can only ask in bewilderment, "Wherefore is this?" - what have I done to deserve this? Antony does not mention what Enobarbus must have told him, only accuses her of what he has actually seen: letting a lackey, an errand boy, kiss her hand. But he feels like a cuckold.

Comment

We know there must be more to it than this: these are the actions of a desperate man. Thidias is no common "fellow"; he is Caesar's accomplished ambassador. But Antony finds himself deserted now by those he has trusted; he has lost his authority and prestige. The slightest hint of Cleopatra's infidelity can throw him into a rage of despair. Thus his reference to "the horned herd" on the "hill of Bason." Bason is a hill cited in the Old Testament (Psalms 22: 12; 68: 15) for its height and for the number of oxen on it. He thinks of himself as the greatest cuckold in the world, because he would "outroar the horned heads." This refers to a popular joke in which a man whose wife was unfaithful was said to grow cuckold's horns.

Feeling so wretched and betrayed, he cannot speak civilly to her who caused it any more than a condemned man can thank the hangman for being handy with his noose. A servant interrupts the violent scene, bringing in Thidias who has been soundly whipped. Antony sends him back to Caesar to make his report and insultingly tells his rival to whip, or hang, or torture Hipparchus one of Antony's freed slaves in exchange.

Comment

North tells us that in abandoning Hipparchus thus to Caesar's mercies, Antony was not condemning an innocent man but "the first of all his infranchised bondmen that revolted from him, and yielded unto Caesar...."

When they are gone, he turns back to Cleopatra, but the fire has died down now. He can reflect that, as our heavenly moon's eclipses portend disasters on earth, so the change in Cleopatra, his earthly moon, "portends alone/ The fall of Antony!" She is all patience, waiting for the fire of his anger to burn itself out. When it has died, she reassures him. If her heart is cold toward him, she swears, let it freeze into hailstones of poison and the first of these kill her slowly as it dissolves; and the second her cherished son Caesarion; and so on till all her children and the people of Egypt be dead and covered with flies. "I am satisfied," he says as she finishes. And with his restored faith comes back some of the old optimism and bounce: "There's hope in't yet," for him. But though his army is pretty much intact and his navy back in shape, he knows he will be battling against odds, so he will give no quarter on the battlefield. And since it may be his last night alive he determines to make it a gaudy, festive one. It is Cleopatra's birthday and they will celebrate it without stint, as in earlier, better times. Off they go, Antony bluffly boasting that next time he fights, he will deal death like the plague itself. Enobarbus remains behind; this scene has decided him. Hesitant before how to act, now he sees his path clear before him. Antony's optimism, he feels, is unwarranted; his courage, foolhardy, "In that mood/ The dove will pack at the estridge [hawk]." He can foresee only doom in Antony's action, for it is based on passion rather than reason. So Enobarbus follows the council of prudence and makes his decision: "I will seek/. Some way to leave him."

Comment

Enobarbus is a hard-headed realist and judges Antony from that point of view. "When valor preys on reason," he says proverbially, "it eats the sword it fights with." In other words, Antony is still torn between what his reason tells him is the wise thing to do and what his passions insist he must do regardless. Prudence or reason should tell him not to fight, at least until his forces are stronger; but his proud heart makes him foolhardy.

SUMMARY

This scene is eventful and rich in characterization. The important events that it chronicles are these:

1. Antony, in desperation, tries to salvage some of the old bravado by challenging Caesar to personal combat and by mistreating his ambassador.

2. Thidias attempts to seduce Cleopatra to Caesar's side, but fails.

3. Cleopatra's deception of Thidias arouses Antony's first suspicions of her disloyalty.

The atmosphere throughout Cleopatra's court is one of defeat and disillusion. Antony is desperate, strikes out wildly because he has lost control of the situation, flails like a groggy boxer. He sees his vast power melting away to a few friends, and even they are no longer to be trusted. Though he manages to hold on and even to come back at the end of this round, he will not survive the next. So Enobarbus, watching his master's dissolution, decides to join the traitors who have already gone over to Caesar. But though he sees clearly Antony being torn apart by the tug of war between reason and passion, he does not realize that a similar war is raging in himself.

ANTONY AND CLEOPATRA

TEXTUAL ANALYSIS

ACT 4

ACT 4, SCENE 1

Caesar, with Agrippa and Maecenas, receives Antony's letter of challenge in his camp and laughs it to scorn. Maecenas estimates Antony's anger to be desperation and urges Caesar to attack his enemy in the heat of it. Caesar concurs that the time is ripe; with so many deserters from Antony's ranks he feels he can win at the odds. He orders a huge celebration feast.

ACT 4, SCENE 2

Antony and his confidants receive Caesar's rebuke. Antony seems honestly perplexed by Caesar's refusal of a duel. Enobarbus explains that his advantage is in numbers, and Antony replies that he will beat him in open battle, too. Then he asks his most loyal lieutenant, "Woo't [Wilt] thou fight well," and Enobarbus says, "I'll strike and cry 'Take all."

Comment

Enobarbus means he will fight to the death, winner take all. The **irony** of his staunchness is that he plans to be fighting on Caesar's side against Antony.

    Antony is pleased by his response and calls for the feast to celebrate Cleopatra's birthday. As his servants answer his summons, he takes each by the hand in what seems a farewell embrace. Cleopatra wonders at it; Enobarbus attributes it to his sorrow. Antony grows maudlin, asking his servants to tend him well at that night's feast for it may be the last time they serve him at all. He may be wounded or killed in tomorrow's battle. So he speaks to them as one who says goodbye, and asks them to tend him in the same spirit. The servants are discomforted by these remarks; they grow uneasy and start to weep, and even Enobarbus says through his tears, "for shame,/ Transform us not to women." This jostles Antony out of his mood; bluff and confident again, he disclaims any sadness. "For I spake to you for your comfort," he says. He hopes well for tomorrow, he claims, for victory not death, and on that rising note bids them to supper and to drink.

ACT 4, SCENE 3

This is another short prelude to the battle that is brewing. A company of Antony's soldiers, standing guard before the palace, are frightened in the middle of their watch by strange music under the earth. At first, they do not know what it signifies, but one of them says it bodes no good. He interprets it to mean that Antony's patron god, Hercules, is leaving him.

Comment

Hercules is a mythological figure famous for his size, strength, and manliness. He is Antony's patron.

They are much agitated and disturbed by this explanation and confer with some other soldiers who also marvel at its strangeness. Then they all cautiously follow to investigate its source.

Comment

Indeed "'tis strange," as one of the soldiers observes. But men and particularly soldiers have at all times and in all places been superstitious and had the natural desire to know ahead of time the outcome of the next day's battle. Such prodigies and prophecies occur frequently in Shakespeare's plays, especially before battles. Compare, for instance, Richard III's visions before Bosworth Field and Brutus's before Philippi. Here the unnatural music is an evil omen of eventual defeat for Antony's forces.

ACT 4, SCENE 4

The night is no more peaceful inside the palace. Antony, anxious for the dawn, cannot sleep. He rises early and calls for Eros to help him put on his armor. When Cleopatra cannot coax him back to bed, she goes to help him dress. But she does not understand the complicated contraption and fumbles with the buckles. Good-naturedly he puts her off; it is not for his body she provides the strength, but for his heart. But she insists on taking a hand, so he shows her the proper way to do it.

Comment

The elaborate armor plate is an **anachronism**. Shakespeare substitutes the Elizabethan full suit of iron for the simple breastplate and greaves of the Romans. What is most touching in the scene is Cleopatra's simplicity. She is no more the queen; she is an anxious wife, fearful for her soldier husband as he leaves for war. And Antony's jovial attempts to cheer her seem forced.

When she succeeds with the stubborn buckle, he half-seriously complains to Eros that his queen makes a defter squire than he. He tries to reassure her about the coming battle. A soldier enters, armed, to fetch the general; and Antony warms to his day's task. The men are ready; trumpets flourish. On come the captains and soldiers; they greet their general. He finishes donning his armor; it is time to go. He turns a moment to say goodbye to Cleopatra. No formal farewell; no "mechanic compliment." With a brief "soldier's kiss" he leaves her "like a man of steel." Then he bids her that gentlest of goodbyes: "Adieu." She turns to Charmian; "he goes forth gallantly," she says and is sure that were he to fight Caesar alone, he would win. "But now ... ?" she worries, as she leaves the scene.

ACT 4, SCENE 5

Trumpets sound through Antony's busy camp. He greets the old soldier who advised him against a naval engagement at Actium (Act 3, Scene 7). Antony regrets not having taken that advice. The soldier reveals that one more has deserted from Antony's ranks: Enobarbus. The general is dumbfounded. Although Eros claims his property and gear are still in camp, the old soldier insists that he has fled. Antony's reaction is surprising. He does not blame his lieutenant, but himself: "O, my fortunes have/ Corrupted honest men." He asks Eros to write a letter to Enobarbus saying "that I wish he never find more cause/ To change a master." Then he sends it along with Enobarbus's abandoned treasure, after him.

ACT 4, SCENE 6

Caesar's camp is no less busy; no fewer trumpets flourish. Caesar enters with Agrippa and Dolabella and the deserter Enobarbus. Caesar gives orders to his troops to take Antony alive. He foresees victory that day and following it a period of universal peace.

Comment

In fact, after the civil wars the Roman Empire was united under Augustus Caesar for an unprecedented period of world peace called the Pax Romana, or Roman Peace.

A messenger announces the arrival of Antony in the field. Caesar gives his battle plan. He orders Agrippa to place all those who have come over from Antony's army in the front ranks so that he will be confused and seem to destroy his own men. They leave Enobarbus alone on stage. He ponders the fate of the others who have deserted to Caesar's side.

Comment

These second thoughts are no doubt natural enough but seem to be brought on by Caesar's battle plan. He is, in effect, using the deserters as so much cushion to absorb the shock of the attack.

Alexas, sent by Antony to confer with Herod, betrayed his master and persuaded the Jewish king to join him, in Caesar's service; and for this Caesar hanged him. Canidius and the rest of the deserters have been given tasks but no trust. "I have done ill," Enobarbus concludes on his betrayal; "I will joy no more." At this moment of moral crisis, he hears that a messenger has arrived with his abandoned treasure and equipment, bearing Antony's farewell note and a bounty besides. Enobarbus thinks he is being mocked at first, but then he is plunged even further into dejection. He contrasts the kindness and generosity with which Antony repays his own treachery, and his heart swells almost to bursting with the thought. "If swift thought break it not, a swifter mean/ Shall outstrike thought," Enobarbus vows, but feels sure that "thought will do't."

Comment

The depression into which Enobarbus sinks is suicidal. Here he vows that if he does not die naturally of a broken heart, his "swifter mean," his sword, will do it surely.

ACT 4, SCENE 7

The stage now represents the battlefield between the two camps, contended for by both armies. First a contingent of Caesar's troops, commanded by Agrippa, retreats across the stage. The battle is not going well for them. Then Antony helps the wounded Scarus to cover.

Comment

We are a little surprised to find Scarus still with Antony. It was he who, after the first defeat at Actium, had almost decided to quit his foundering lord, and along with Canidius go over to Caesar's side (Act 3, Scene 10). Here he has fought valiantly for Antony.

Though concerned over Scarus's wounds, the men are able to joke about their victory, Scarus says that his wound "was like a T,/ But now 'tis made an H."

Comment

Another cut has been added across the bottom of the T to make an H sideways (I). There also may be a pun on the pronunciation of "H", ("aitch"), which in Shakespeare's time was closer to "ache."

"We'll beat 'em into the bench-holes," Scarus boasts.

Comment

"Bench-holes" refers to the seat holes in privies or outhouses. "I have yet/ Room for six scotches more," does not refer to his drinking capacity, but to his ability to endure wounds.

Eros comes on to rally them after the retreating foe as the scene closes.

ACT 4, SCENE 8

The battle is over; Antony's formations return victorious to their camp under the walls of Alexandria. Antony congratulates them and gives them encouragement for the next day's battle, when they will annihilate the enemy. They have fought like Hectors, he compliments them.

Comment

Hector was the hero who defended Troy against the Greeks in Homer's Iliad.

Cleopatra rushes on to greet her victorious husband. He addresses her as "Thou day o' the world," and sweeps her into his embrace, harnessed in iron though he is. "Leap thou," he commands her, "to my heart ..." His high spirits spill over into jokes about his age and prowess, and he even offers to Scarus's lips the hand he was so jealous of the day before. He orders his men back into formation; calls to the trumpeters for a flourish, and a roll from the drums, and marches his army off in triumph through the city.

ACT 4, SCENE 9

The triumphal clamor of Antony's camp dies into the gloomy watchfulness of Caesar's. A group of sentries on the outskirts of the camp come upon Enobarbus spilling the last torment of despair from his soul. He calls upon the moon - "the sovereign mistress of true melancholy" - to witness his remorse for having betrayed his beloved lord. He wishes that the damp night air will poison him and be his death, a punishment for his infamous revolt against Antony.

Comment

Enobarbus calls the moon "mistress of true melancholy" because it was once generally thought to cause mental disorders or lunacy-from the Latin word for moon, luna. It was also believed that at night the moon, like a sponge, sucked up the dew from the earth, into a miasma or poisonous vapor which caused disease. In his guilt and despair Enobarbus begs the moon to "disponge" this poison on him.

Then begging Antony's forgiveness, he dies of a broken heart with his friend's name upon his lips. The watchmen of the guard, approaching to question him, are puzzled to find him dead. Suddenly they hear reveille mustering the troops; it is the signal that their tour of duty is over. They carry the dead man off to the guard-room.

Comment

It is ironical that Enobarbus, the hard-headed realist, should die so sentimentally, by moonlight from a broken heart. The **irony** points up a basic conflict in Enobarbus' character; he is a soft-hearted cynic.

ACT 4, SCENES 10-12

Again we are on the battlefield between the two camps. A new day is breaking; the generals draw up their battleplans. First Antony and Scarus march across with their army. Antony says that Caesar, frightened to meet him again on land after yesterday's defeat, prepares for a naval engagement. Antony orders his foot-soldiers to take up positions on the hills commanding the city, from which they can follow the progress of the sea battle. His ships have already put to sea.

Comment

Line 7 is usually construed as incomplete; the passage does not seem to make complete sense. But if "order for sea is given,/ They have put forth the haven," is put in parentheses, then "where," line 8, can refer to "hills" and some sense be made of it. "On foot" in this case refers most probably to the foot-soldiers actually with them.

When they have gone to find their vantage point, Caesar leads his army on. He resolves that, unless he is attacked on land, he will depend that day on his seapower to win the advantage. With Antony already in command of the hills, he orders his soldiers into the valleys. When they have gone, the stage remains empty for a few moments, while an alarm, "as at a sea-fight," rises in the distance and then dies down again. When all is quiet once more, Antony comes on with Scarus.

Comment

The sea-battle has been joined, but Antony and Scarus are so far inland and so busy looking for a place from which to watch it, that they are unaware of the noise.

Antony spots a good vantage point further up by a tall pine tree and leaves Scarus alone on stage while he goes off to observe the battle. When he is alone, Scarus reveals that all is not well; he expects disaster that day, for "swallows have built/ In Cleopatra's sails their nests," and that is an evil omen. Although the augurers (soothsayers who could predict the future from signs and omens) say they do not know what this means, they show by their grim looks and their silence that it bodes no good. Antony too is moody, shifting unsteadily from hope to fear, from courage to dejection. Scarus's soliloquy is interrupted by a frantic Antony: "All is lost," he exclaims, and immediately accuses Cleopatra of betraying him. For his men, when they had sailed out of the harbor, instead of attacking the enemy fleet joined them, surrendered themselves, tossed their caps in the air and caroused together "like friends long lost." Antony's defeat is complete; he gives over utterly to thoughts of despair and death. But he promises to get even with the "triple-turn'd whore" who has sold him out "to this novice," as he contemptuously refers to Caesar.

Comment

Antony is accusing Cleopatra of being unfaithful three times: (1) She went from Julius Caesar to Gnaeus Pompey; (2) from Pompey to Antony; (3) and now from Antony to Octavius Caesar.

He cares for nothing now-loyalty, friends, nothing-but revenging himself on the enchantress who has cast her charm over him; and then his own death, for he no longer wants to live. The friends (or rather those he thought were friends, and Cleopatra chief among them) who were as slavishly devoted as spaniels to him when he was master, now abandon him: to "melt their sweets on blossoming Caesar." He is like a great pine tree that once towered over the forest and now is stripped of its bark and branches and left to decay.

Comment

Antony falls because his friends leave him. Their betrayal is both cause and characteristic of his downfall; the play's action and characters and **imagery** are based upon it. There are many betrayals, from those whose allegiance is prompted merely by political advantage to those whose loyalty and devotion are almost their only reason for existing. Conquered kings leave Antony after the first defeat; then closer supporters like Canidius; finally, the closest, most trusted of all: Enobarbus. This is at the very core of that soldier's character (he sees it plainly in Antony, but not in himself): the conflict between his head and his heart, between the counsels of prudence and the ties of affection. So the action of the play is finally decided by the mass surrender of Antony's mutinous navy, without a sword bared to fight. And finally, Antony's doubt of Cleopatra's loyalty and his fear that she has sold him out to Caesar bring on the tragic events which end the play: his suicide and hers shortly following. This idea of Antony's being stripped of his followers and friends as his fortunes decline is expressed in the **imagery** of the play also. Many times he refers to the treachery of those who have revolted. In the very first act, both he and Caesar speak of the fickleness of the common people's love for their leaders. Once Antony compared his lost honor to a great tree left branchless (Act 3, Scene 4). Here again, in his ultimate dishonor he speaks of himself as stripped of his bark and branches; the "friends" of his better days like spaniels have followed their fortunes to Caesar's camp. There is a kind of raw justice in his thus being abandoned; for his first and overriding fault was to abandon his own world-Rome and its values, his family and friends-for Cleopatra's sake. The wheel of fortune has come full turn.

Again he blames "this false soul of Egypt," this "right gipsy," who has cheated and beguiled him.

Comment

"Gipsy" is a play on the original meaning of the word. The name was derived from a corruption of the word "Egyptian," since gipsies were thought in medieval times to come from Egypt. A gipsy was also commonly thought of as a cheat. "Fast and loose" is the proverbial name for a cheating game, or trickery.

He calls for his faithful lieutenant; but Cleopatra answers his call. He is repulsed by the sight of her, but she does not understand his anger. In a torment of rage he sweeps over her, drowning her in abuse. Let Caesar take her back to Rome in his triumphal procession, a shameful mockery, a whore, to be displayed like a monster in a cage. Let Octavia have her for awhile to dull her nails on Cleopatra's face. The frightened queen runs before this wave of hatred which threatens to engulf her.

Comment

Antony seems uncertain as to what would be his best revenge on Cleopatra. He can kill her outright, as it almost seems at times he must do, swept to it by his rage. But in other, cooler moments he thinks the sharper pain would be to abandon her to Caesar and let her be degraded as his captive-which would be not one, but many deaths.

She is gone, but he cannot reconcile himself. The rage upon him is like Nessus' legendary shirt of fire which tortured Hercules to his destruction.

Comment

To revenge a wound, Nessus, the centaur, gave Dejanira, Hercules' wife, a shirt dyed with his own blood to be used as a love charm. The shirt caused Hercules' painful death. Lichas brought the deadly garment to Hercules, and for his pains was thrown into the sea. Alcides is another name for Hercules, after his ancestor Alcaeus. It is plain that Antony thinks of himself as Hercules here.

Hercules is Antony's patron among the gods, so in his misery the defeated general prays to him for strength. Then the accumulated anger and humiliation overcome him and he swears "the witch shall die." Thus sworn, he leaves to find Eros.

SUMMARY

Of course, this is Antony's fateful scene. The second naval defeat not only undoes his victory of the day before, but the surrender of his fleet without a fight convinces him of Cleopatra's betrayal. He sees his own death by suicide clearly before him, but wants first to inflict some punishment upon Cleopatra. He is not clear at first what form his revenge will take, but after meeting her and scaring her off by his fury, he decides she must die, and goes off to find her.

ACT 4, SCENE 13

Meanwhile Cleopatra is frightened for her life by Antony's furious attack. She does not understand the reasons for it, and runs to her attendants for protection. "He's more mad/ Than Telamon for his shield," she laments.

Comment

When the Greek champion Achilles was killed before Troy his famous shield and armor were to be given to the bravest of the Greeks. Telamon Ajax went mad from disappointment when Odysseus was chosen instead of himself. "The boar of Thessaly/ Was never so emboss'd," refers to a legendary wild boar sent in revenge by Diana, goddess of the hunt, to ravage Thessaly. "Emboss'd" probably means foaming at the mouth from exertion.

Charmian devises a plan. Cleopatra will go to the mausoleum she has already prepared for her entombment and lock herself in. Meanwhile she will send Mardian, her eunuch, to tell Antony she is dead. She does so, saying she has killed herself.

Comment

Cleopatra is true to her character to the end. She adds to her instructions to Mardian: "And bring me how he takes my death to the monument."

ACT 4, SCENE 14

Back in Cleopatra's palace, empty now but for Eros and himself, Antony's passion has subsided. His dejection is still profound-he will not come out of it again-but he is more reflective than furious now. He opens his conversation with a strange question: "Eros, thou yet beholds't me?" "Ay, noble lord," his bewildered friend replies. Antony is comparing himself and his fortunes to clouds that race across the evening sky. As we watch, the clouds assume various shapes, one looks like a dragon, another like a bear, a lion, a turreted castle, a cliff; a mountain, "a blue promontory with trees upon't."

The clouds no sooner take a shape-say, a horse-when they dissolve again back into nothing, "as water is in water." So, the defeated Antony reflects, am I "even such a body." He too will dissolve, like so much vapor. He went to war for Egypt's queen, because he loved her and thought she loved him. He thought he had a million loyal friends: all gone, dissolved. She has dealt from a stacked deck and played his cards into Caesar's hand. Now he is trumped. But, he comforts the weeping Eros, they still have a way out; "there is left us/ Ourselves to end ourselves." Upon this quiet scene comes Mardian with Cleopatra's false message to shock Antony back into anger. "O' thy vile lady!" he exclaims upon seeing him, "She has robb'd me of my sword."

Comment

Antony's "sword" here as elsewhere in the play stands for his manhood, power, all that he was before he fell in with Cleopatra.

Mardian denies it, protests his mistress's love and loyalty: he uses the past tense. Antony vows Cleopatra's death before Mardian lies that she is already dead. Not only dead, but by her own hand, and in despair for having lost Antony, with his name the last thought in her heart. When he hears this false message, all the life goes out of him. He has been living only to punish Cleopatra; now that he thinks she is dead, there is no more reason for him to go on. He starts to remove his armor, as if for sleep.

Comment

There is a double meaning in Antony's "Unarm, Eros, the long day's task is done and we must sleep," as he removes his armor. The sleep he refers to is not physical rest but the sleep of death. This parallel between the passage from light into dark, day into night, and the decline from life into death is repeated several times in the final scenes. It is repeated by Antony later - "the torch is out" - and is picked up by Cleopatra and her maids: Act 4, Scene 15, Lines 9-10, 85; Act 5, Scene 2, Lines 80, 192-193.

Eros helps him; he cannot get it off fast enough. Finally, the uniform of his soldiery stripped, he sends Eros out with the "bruised pieces," while he prepares for death. Now he will be reconciled with his queen in that world beyond death "where souls do couch on flowers." Hand in hand they will walk like lovers so as to steal the show even from Dido and her Aeneas.

Comment

Dido and Aeneas are famous lovers from Book Four of Virgil's *Aeneid*. When Aeneas left her to sail for Italy, she killed herself. Later, visiting Avernus, the infernal regions, he saw her again with her husband, Sichaeus.

He calls Eros back into the room. Remember, he says, you have sworn, when the need should come, when death is the only alternative to disgrace and horror, you would kill me. "Do't, the time is come ..." he commands. Eros turns pale at the thought; but Antony shows him the alternative: to see his master brought back to Rome disgraced, a captured slave behind Caesar's chariot. Again he exacts Eros's oath to kill him, and this time Eros complies.

He draws his sword; he tells Antony to turn his face aside, and when he has done so Eros plunges the sword into himself! "Thus I do escape the sorrow/ Of Antony's death," he exclaims. This is Antony's second example: Cleopatra and Eros have both shown him the way. Without more delay he draws his sword and falls on it, but the wound is not immediately fatal. A guard comes in followed by Decretas, and he begs them to finish the job. But they are all frightened to see their leader fallen, and refuse. Decretas, when the guard has fled, pulls the bloody sword from Antony's wound but not to answer his prayer. He intends instead to use it as his passport into Caesar's good graces. Diomedes enters looking for Antony. Decretas, hiding the bloody sword beneath his cloak, points to the dying man and leaves. And now, too late, Diomedes reveals that Cleopatra is not dead but locked in her monument and fearful that just this would happen as the result of her lies. With the last of his ebbing strength Antony summons his guard and as his last command bids them take him to Cleopatra. Weeping, they take him up and carry him off.

SUMMARY

In these final tragic scenes, Shakespeare's dramatic power is at its highest. This scene moves inexorably from event to event as Antony seeks his death.

1. Antony reflects on the vagaries of fortune, the dream-like quality of a life which can change so suddenly and so drastically. He is stoically determined to end his own sufferings.

2. Mardian delivers the false message of Cleopatra's death, but does not try to persuade Antony of her innocence.

3. This knowledge frees Antony for his own death. Still thinking her guilty of betraying him, he seeks his mistress in the afterlife to beg her pardon. For he is sure of their immortality.

4. After Eros kills himself rather than bear that sword against his lord, Antony's suicide is unsuccessful. Nor will his soldiers finish it for him.

5. Decretas steals the bloody sword to show Caesar and win his friendship.

6. Dying, Antony learns from Diomedes that Cleopatra still lives and still loves him. But there is no tragic **irony** in this knowledge that comes too late; Antony would not have been saved. Unlike Romeo, whose suicide is similarly based on the mistaken belief that his lover is dead, Antony's doom is inevitable. All that keeps him alive is his passion to punish Cleopatra; once he believes she is beyond the reach of his revenge, he is reconciled with her again. His discovery that she still lives merely allows that reconciliation to take place on this side of the grave.

ACT 4, SCENE 15

Locked in her monument, Cleopatra complains to Charmian; she fears she will never leave her tomb. Charmian is attempting, unsuccessfully, to comfort her, when Diomedes returns with the dying Antony, borne by his guards. Cleopatra had feared he was dead, but how much more fearful is the reality of a dying Antony to the mere thought of a dead one. Surely the sun must burn up the heavens at this calamity and leave the world in darkness.

> Comment

Her figure of speech is based on the Ptolemaic astronomy, which conceived of the sun as a planet whirling around a fixed earth in a hollow sphere (see above, Act 2, Scene 7). If the sphere were burnt up, the sun would fly off into space and the earth grow dark. Then the varying light and darkness of the heavens would sink into perpetual night.

Her lover's name breaks from her lips in anguish when she sees him wounded; she cries to those around her to help her lift him up into the monument. But he puts her fears at naught: it was not Caesar's hand produced this wound, but his own.

> Comment

Cleopatra's urgency and Antony's reply seem to indicate that she is afraid Antony has been wounded by Caesar and pursued by him. He tells her he is in no danger of being captured. Later she will refuse to open the door of her mausoleum out of fear of being captured, and will insist on hauling her dying lover up to her.

"I am dying, Egypt, dying," he tells her, and begs one final kiss, but she is afraid to leave her sanctuary, lest she become Caesar's "brooch," or trophy. She has already decided to die there by knife, drugs, or, significantly, serpent. So with the help of her maids and his guards, she manages to lift Antony into the monument.

> Comment

Cleopatra and her maids probably occupied the balcony over the Elizabethan inner stage. This was used to represent balconies, "the heavens," all high places, or to house the musicians. The women's efforts to raise Antony are extremely moving: remember that women's parts were played by young boys. Their difficulties were not pretense.

Again in his lover's arms, Antony repeats, "I am dying, Egypt, dying." "Die when thou hast lived" again, she says, brought back to life by her kisses. But he has not much strength left. He must use it to admonish her. He gives her three cautions. First, that she should not sacrifice her honor to Caesar in order to secure her safety. Second, that she should trust none of Caesar's advisers and lieutenants but Proculeius. She replies that she need not trust even him: her own hands and resolution will be enough. Third, that she ought not to mourn over his death, but glory in the nobility of his life who was "the greatest prince o' the world …" For he did not die basely, nor cowardly, but nobly by the hand of another Roman - "valiantly vanquished." That is all: three words of advice and he is dead in his mistress's arms: thus "the crown o' the earth doth melt." And in the almost superhuman eloquence of her grief she exclaims, "O, wither'd is the garland of the war,/ The soldier's pole is fall'n: young boys and girls/ Are level now with men: the odds is gone,/ And there is nothing left remarkable/ Beneath the visiting moon." With that she swoons.

Comment

"Soldier's pole" is variously interpreted according to what "pole" means. (1) If it refers to a flag or banner, it means the standard which leads them into battle. (2) If it refers to the northern pole star or lodestar, which is the constant in the compass, it means the norm by which a soldier is to be measured. This echoes the remark of the second guard in Scene 14, "The star is fall'n."

"The odds is gone" means there is no standard left by which to separate the men from the boys, children from adults.

Iras is thrown into a violet agitation by her mistress's fainting spell. She calls upon her as "Royal Egypt: Empress!" until Charmian cries "Peace, peace, Iras!" Cleopatra revives saying, "No more but e'en a woman," like any, the simplest of her sex. What meaning is there left in titles or distinctions when Antony is dead? "All's but nought …" Patience or impatience to bear such suffering are equally meaningless. "Then is it sin," she asks herself, "To rush into the secret house of death/ Ere death come to us?"

Comment

The sudden and strange calmness that comes over Cleopatra in the midst of her anguish comes from her settled decision to kill herself. This will remove all of her sufferings, take her out of Caesar's hands as well, and reunite her with her love. Thus she repeats the image used earlier by Antony, "The torch is out," in Scene 14, line 46: "Our lamp is spent," she says to her waiting women, "it's out." They have but to bury Antony and die "after the high Roman fashion," i.e., by their own hands.

SUMMARY

This is recognized as one of the great death scenes in dramatic literature. Its greatness lies partly in the greatness of its characters, partly in the pathos of their love. We are not allowed to forget their greatness, though they are reduced by circumstance almost to absurdity. Analyzed coldly, the scene would be ludicrous. A man who has tried to kill himself, by mistake, and botched the job, is hauled up the side of his mistress's tomb by a bunch of her women because she is too frightened to open the door. But the characters are never allowed to become ridiculous; we do not laugh. We are reminded of who they are by Antony's calling her "Egypt" rather than Cleopatra, and by his concern that she should remember, not the miserable twilight of his career, but its blazing noon. He is jealous of honor even in death. And Cleopatra has never been more queenly than in mourning him. She is strengthened by his death much as he had been earlier by the report of hers. The calm that settles over her is accentuated by the panic of her waiting-women. She looks forward to death as he had; all else becomes meaningless. There is nothing more in life to interest her but leaving it.

ANTONY AND CLEOPATRA

TEXTUAL ANALYSIS

ACT 5

ACT 5, SCENE 1

The scene shifts from the still depths of a doomed love to the efficient bustle of Caesar's camp, flushed with his recent triumph. A council of war is in progress. Caesar cockily dispatches Dolabella to demand Antony's surrender as Decretas enters, carrying the blood-stained sword of Antony. He passes himself off as Antony's loyal follower: "I wore my life/ To spend upon his haters." Now he offers his services - and his loyalty - to Caesar and promises to do the same for him: "As I was to him/ I'll be to Caesar." For, he explains, "Antony is dead." Caesar is surprised and genuinely moved. So great a **catastrophe**, he says, "should make a greater crack," should cause some similar **catastrophe** in "the round world."

Comment

The philosophical basis of ancient and medieval thought (and up to Shakespeare's time) about the natural world was that all objects and events, including man, were held together by bands of sympathetic magic and analogy. When some great moral evil was committed, it was thought to shake the foundations of nature, and its reverberations were felt in natural disasters. So, too, prodigies of nature were thought to presage or prophesy the fate of men. (See, for example, *Julius Caesar*, Act 1, Scene 3; or *Macbeth*, Act 2, Scene 4.)

For Antony's death is not just his personal tragedy; it alters that entire part of the world which he ruled. Caesar is saddened to hear it, and exchanges reminiscences of Antony's exploits with his advisors. "Say nothing of the dead but what is good," the Roman aphorism admonished, and their remarks are in keeping with its spirit. Agrippa reflects stoically that the gods who make men make them flawed so they will not challenge their supremacy. What makes the news specially poignant to Caesar is the knowledge that he has hounded Antony to this deed. He has cut Antony off as he would a diseased part of his body, not in despite or hatred, but to keep the sound part wholesome. It was him or Antony; the world held not room enough for both. Then Caesar launches into a stirring eulogy of his defeated "brother," "competitor" (friendly rival), "mate in empire," "friend and companion in the front of war,/ Arm of mine own body and the heart where mine his thoughts did kindle." He blames their falling out, which has led them to this moment, on the influence of their guiding stars, doomed to opposition.

> **Comment**

There is a natural bond among Shakespeare's great men, that does not hold them to men of lesser rank, the ordinary people. They can be better than most men; and when they are bad, they are always worse. But, good or bad, they remain alone, isolated by their stature like great trees. Caesar here feels this. He eulogizes Antony as once Antony eulogized the dead Brutus on the scarred field of Philippi, because he recognizes that a great man may fall from grace, but never from greatness.

Caesar abruptly breaks off his sorrowful praise of Antony to question an Egyptian messenger, sent by Cleopatra to learn of Caesar's intentions and accept his instructions. Caesar tells her not to worry: he will act honorably toward her and kindly. "For Caesar cannot live to be ungentle.' Immediately he turns to Proculeius and orders him to reassure the Egyptian queen of his good intentions, "Lest, in her greatness, by some mortal stroke/ She do defeat us."

> **Comment**

Caesar knows the caliber of his enemy. He reassures Cleopatra because her suicide will spoil his plans for a triumphal return to Rome. She is the trophy of this war; if he can bring her back alive his fame will be eternal.

Evidently concerned by this last thought he sends Gallus along to back up Proculeius and bids them a speedy return. Then he invites those closest to him who remain to hear the story of how and why this war came about.

ANTONY AND CLEOPATRA

SUMMARY

This scene contains two important events:

1. Caesar and his followers learn of Antony's death and lament it.

2. Caesar devises a stratagem to take Cleopatra alive. The first event puts Caesar in a favorable light; the audience has just been deeply moved by Antony's death and feels receptive to Caesar's eulogy. The tragic effect depends upon our admiration of the tragic hero. He cannot be thought of as completely evil or we will not be sorry for him. Caesar's eulogy helps make of Antony's tragic fall a truly cosmic **catastrophe**. But Cleopatra's sending a messenger to seek Caesar's instructions may seem puzzling. When last we saw her she was bent on death; now she seems bent on currying Caesar's favor. We will learn later that her purpose is to secure one promise from Caesar before she dies: that her son Caesarion (Octavius Caesar's half-brother) will wear the crown of Egypt after her. Caesar's reply to her puts him in a bad light. Nothing is further from the audience's sympathy at this point than his attempt to beguile her in her grief and add to her torment. It is typical of Caesar that he can move so easily and unselfconsciously from the noble sentiment to the base.

Act 5, Scene 2

Just as Antony, before he commits suicide, reflects upon the insecurity of life that changes so quickly from prosperity to disaster, so Cleopatra opens the scene in which she will die. Since life is full of treacheries, hopes which are never fulfilled, misfortunes without meaning, changes for the worse - then suicide, which puts an end to all uncertainty, is a "better life." And so, she seeks "that thing that ends all other deeds": death.

Comment

She says that death "sleeps and never palates more the dung,/ The beggar's nurse, and Caesar's." She confuses suicide with the state that it produces. In death the beggar and the emperor are equally free of the "dung" of mortal life. Compare Antony's speech in Act 1, Scene 1: "Our dungy earth alike/ Feeds beast as man ..." in which he celebrates passionate love as that which separates men from beasts. Here, that love perished, Cleopatra seeks escape from "our dungy earth" through death. "Nurse" here means "wet-nurse," one who suckles an infant.

Proculeius breaks in upon her morbid reflections with Caesar's message. This is the man Antony told her to trust; but she has no use for him now. She asks her price: "Give me conquered Egypt for my son ..." But her attitude toward her conqueror is host le and aloof: she treats his messenger coldly with a "take-it-or-leave-it" tone. Though defeated, she will not give in. Proculeius tries to win her confidence. He tells her, in effect, she will catch more flies with honey than with vinegar. "Let me report to him/ Your sweet dependency," he says, and you'll find him begging you for suggestions how best to please you.

Comment

"Pray in aid" is a legal phrase meaning to ask for advice or assistance on some question.

She softens somewhat, shows her obedience to him, and asks to see him. Proculeius, gladdened by her change of tone, is about to deliver her request when a troop of soldiers, led by Gallus, surprises them from behind and surrounds the monument. He tells Proculeius and the soldiers to guard her till Caesar comes.

Comment

Now Caesar's purpose in backing Proculeius up is clear. He sends the trusted messenger to put Cleopatra off her guard and follows up with Gallus and his soldiers to catch her by surprise. He is determined to take her alive.

Immediately upon seeing the soldiers, Cleopatra's waiting women, Iras and Charmian, panic. Cleopatra is cooler-headed. She is determined not to be taken alive. She draws a concealed dagger and is about to kill herself when Proculeius lunges for her arm and manages to wrest the knife away before she can use it. He insists again that she mistakes Caesar's intentions: he means her no harm. Nor does death, she replies, that puts injured dogs out of their misery. Proculeius's tone becomes firmer; he reprimands her for jealously trying to deny Caesar an opportunity to show his generosity. For if she is dead, to whom can he show it? But Cleopatra is distraught. Her accumulated misery breaks out in an anguished cry for death to comfort her. She will have death, she vows, if not from a dagger, then from hunger and thirst and lack of sleep. "This mortal house [her body] I'll ruin,/ Do Caesar what he can." She would prefer the vilest, most painful death to t at which she could never tolerate: the mockery and censure of Rome's vulgar mobs. Dolabella, another of Caesar's diplomats, arrives to relieve Proculeius, whom Caesar wants to see. Proculeius, genuinely concerned for Cleopatra, asks if he may not deliver some message from her. "Say, I would die," she answers. When he is gone, Dolabella tries to break the ice by introducing himself as an old acquaintance. But Cleopatra could not be less inclined to social amenities. She treats him like any uncouth ruffian who will "laugh when boys and women tell their dreams ..." For life seems like a sleep to her now, and the past all a dream, Antony a dream. "O such another sleep," she exclaims, longing for death, "that I might see/ But such another man!" This exclamation loosens a landslide of emotion; words of love and praise for her dead lord pour from her mouth around the bewildered Dolabella. He was like a constellation of stars in the heavens, she says; he was like the great Colossus bestriding the ocean; "his rear'd arm crested the world"; his voice was like the music of the heavenly spheres to those he loved, but those he hated, like "the rattling thunder." His generosity knew no barrenness of winter; he gave like an autumn harvest. Even his delights were so enormous they raised him out of the common sea of pleasure, as dolphins show their backs above the element they live in. He had kings for servants, and kingdoms and islands, were like small change "dropp'd from his pocket."

Comment

The picture Cleopatra imagines of Antony is of a huge giant, his head in the heavens, striding across the earth, spanning oceans, dropping islands like coins as he goes. This is what she was imagining when she complained at Antony's death: "Young boys and girls/ Are level now with men: the odds is gone ..." Line 84, "the tuned spheres," refers to the Ptolemaic astronomy which taught that the seven spheres of the heavens were made to musical proportions like strings or reeds in an instrument, so that when they moved past each other they produced harmonious melody.

Dolabella is both perplexed and annoyed by her running on. He interrupts her several times but cannot stop her. Finally she asks him if he thinks such a dream could come true. When he says no, she protests loudly. If ever Antony lived, he was greater than her dream. Nature cannot produce men as great as we imagine them, she says, but Antony was nature's masterpiece, greater than any dream or imagination. Dolabella tries to quiet her. He tells her the greatness of her grief not only argues the greatness of her loss, but makes even him grieve deeply over Antony's death. This does quiet her; she trusts Dolabella. "Know you what Caesar means to do with me?" she asks. This puts him in an awkward position: He hates to have to tell her, but he thinks she should know. He starts by defending Caesar's honor; but she saves him embarrassment by saying it for him: "He'll lead me then in triumph." Dolabella admits she is right, as a flourish sounds announcing Caesar's arrival. With him are Proceuleius, Gallus, Maecenas, and some other attendants. Caesar enters, asking, "Which is the Queen of Egypt?"

Comment

His question shows a certain insensibility that is part of Caesar's character. Perhaps it is due to his youth and lack of experience, perhaps to an innate lack of preception. But neither of his diplomatic errand boys, Proculeius or Dolabella, mistook Cleopatra for her maids, or doubted for an instant which of the women was the Queen of Egypt. On the other hand, Caesar is being very politic by using that title. He hopes to put her at her ease by showing her that he still considers her the Queen.

Cleopatra, playing along with his stratagem, falls to her knees in respect and obedience. He protests that she should not kneel; they are equals. He holds no grudges against her for the war, he says, though injured by it. She does not try to defend her actions or excuse them; she blames them on the frailties of her sex. Caesar reassures her of his kind intentions, if she cooperates. But if she tries to defeat him by taking Antony's course of suicide, he will destroy her children. He prepares to leave. Anxious to create a good impression, Cleopatra hands him an account of her wealth before he goes. In it are listed all the major items of her wealth: money, silver and gold plate, jewels. She summons Seleucus, her treasurer, to swear it is accurate. But he does not! He claims the account is fraudulent; she has kept back as much as she has made known. Cleopatra blushes-from shame or rage we cannot tell. But Caesar takes it in good spirit and even approves her business acumen. This does not subdue her anger. She lashes out at Seleucus as an ingrate, a slave she has raised to a position of trust, who now turns on her and curries favor with Caesar because she has been defeated by him. Seleucus recoils from her as she lunges for his eyes. Caesar comes between the two to restrain her. She turns to him, all apology and explanation. She has kept out a few trifles, she admits, unimportant things of no value to give as presents to her common followers and servants, and a few more expensive things to win the friendship of Octavia and Livia, Caesars wife.

Comment

By mentioning these women and their favor, Cleopatra cleverly deceives Caesar into believing that she desires to live and expects to see Rome. This has led some critics to believe that the whole **episode** with Seleucus was purposely staged for Caesar's benefit, perhaps even rehearsed. For if Cleopatra intends to commit suicide, why does she go to the trouble of giving Caesar an account of her assets and withholding some? The same question came up in the previous scene. If she is bent on death, why does Cleopatra try to curry favor with her conqueror? Perhaps the same reason holds here: for the sake of her children. But even so, her concern does not prevent her from throwing them upon Caesar's mercy when she kills herself.

But Seleucus exaggerates out of envy for her, she petulantly accuses him. He should rather have pity on me, she says, as she banishes him from her sight. For the leader is blamed for what his underlings do, and when he falls from grace he is punished for other's faults.

Comment

This statement is a concise theory of classical tragedy, which was supposed to inspire pity and fear in the audience by depicting the fall of a great man. It is the hero's greatness that makes him stand out as a scapegoat or sacrifice for the sins of others; and in his capacity to suffer greatly he is tragic.

Caesar tells her to put her account away; he wants none of her treasure. She continues to wrong him in estimation, he objects; he is no merchant: he will treat her as she herself dictates. "Feed and sleep," he counsels her, having in mind her threat to Proculeius earlier to starve herself. She goes to kneel once more in respect as he leaves, but he restrains her and bids her "adieu." As soon as Caesar is out of sight, Cleopatra drops the mask of meekness and subservience. She has seen through his kindness to the evil design behind it, and she rejects both in the only way left open to her.

Comment

Even the usually unstable Iras seems stolidly resigned to her death. "Finish, good lady," she says, "the bright day is done,/ And we are for the dark." Although this knots up one of the dominant threads of **imagery** in the play, it seems inconsistent for Iras to utter it. Light and dark, day and night, have been used often as emblems of life and death in the play. Antony's downfall and death is described as a passage from day into night. So this line describes a similar fate for Cleopatra and her maids. But it seems improbable that Iras understands all that when she says it. For later, after Dolabella leaves, Cleopatra goes out of her way to frighten Iras with the prospect of returning to Rome as Caesar's captives. Her reason for making the alternative so gruesome is to strengthen Iras's characteristically weak resolve to die. And Iras seems at that point to have no intention of dying. For rather than see her own dishonor she vows to put out, not her life, but her eyes.

Cleopatra whispers instructions to Charmian and sends her off on an errand.

Comment

She has already prepared the means of her death. Plutarch reports that she experimented with various poisons and drugs to discover the properties of each. She found that the bite of an asp brought on death with the greatest speed and least pain. It is evident in this scene that she sends Charmian past the Roman guard to fetch her the asp she already provided for her suicide.

Charmian passes Dolabella on the way out. He has come back secretly to tell her Caesar's plans. The conqueror intends to return to Rome by way of Syria. In three days he will send her and her children before him. Then this last man bows out of the life of a woman who has charmed many men.

Comment

The great charmer's power to win men has not diminished. When Dolabella first met her, earlier in this scene, he had to introduce himself to her. But he has been so moved by her grief and her grandeur that now he risks all to bring her Caesar's confidential plans.

Cleopatra rehearses again for Iras's sake the fate that awaits them in Rome. She reminds her servant of the vulgar rabble who will witness their disgrace, the foul breaths that will mock and jibe at them, the venal officers of the law who will snatch at them like strumpets, the dirty songs that will be sung about them. Comedians will make jokes about them, little scenes will be performed to mock them.

Comment

The reception she foresees in Rome is actually a description of what might happen in Shakespeare's London. The "Egyptian puppet" refers to popular Elizabethan puppet shows: the "mechanic slaves" are tradesmen with their dirty aprons and tools; the "lectors" were minor Roman officials here equated with the London "beadle," a law officer who dealt with prostitutes; hack writers composed **ballads** and sang them about the latest scandalous news: and the quick comedians extemporized farces in the London theatres and courtyards. The word which best betrays the scene Shakespeare is imagining is the verb "boy." Cleopatra is repelled that some boy will take part in the extempore farce. Boys took the women's parts on London stages because women were forbidden there until 1663. But this reference serves another, more important purpose, since it is a boy who, acting Cleopatra's part, squeaks this line out. Shakespeare is here purposely calling the audience's attention to this being only a play, the great queen only a boy actor. By puncturing any pretense, he makes his actors' limitations less noticeable: He strengthens his dramatic illusion by calling attention to its weakness.

With Iras now in a state of near-panic at the prospect of being taken alive to Rome, Charmian returns from her errand. She is no sooner back but Cleopatra sends her with Iras to fetch her royal robes, and her sign of office - the crown of Egypt. She wants to look as beautiful and seductive for this last meeting with Mark Antony as she had her first on the river Cydnus (Act 2, Scene 2). Now Shakespeare interrupts Cleopatra's morbid preparations with a humorous exchange, between the queen who is bent on death and a rustic clown who brings her a basket of figs in which are concealed the poisonous asps by whose bite she will die.

Comment

She has prepared the asps beforehand. She disguises her intent with the rural fellow and his figs in order to allay any suspicion on the part of the guards. We should read this scene after Caesar's departure as the inevitable working-out of Cleopatra's suicidal design. She is resolved to die: not even her conference with Caesar could sway her. "I am marble-constant," she says, "now the fleeting moon/ No planet is of mine." This evocation of the moon knots up the **imagery** of fickleness, changeability, in her character and throughout the play. She is no longer Isis, moongoddess, patroness of fertility and sex. She is now the very image of death and the tranquility it brings. Death puts an end to the vagaries and disappointments of life; after death there are no changes for the worse.

The clown gives up his burden reluctantly and with many warnings and cautions about the "worm of Nilus," the asp. He says that he heard all about how deadly and painful its bite is from a lady who had died from one. Cleopatra is rather impatient with his inane joking. She tries to get rid of him quickly. But he is either too stubborn or too stupid to take her none-too-gentle hints.

Comment

Shakespeare often introduces a scene of low comedy in the midst of serious, even tragic events. His reasons were probably these: (1) It relaxes the tension that might otherwise break into laughter at the wrong time. (2) It provides a sudden contrast which makes the serious events seem even more tragic.

The clown leaves, wishing the queen "joy of the worm." Charmian and Iras reenter, bearing Cleopatra's robes, royal crown, and jewels. She bids her maids attire her as for a state occasion; she is impatient at their slowness.

> Comment

Compare the scene in which Antony commits suicide (Act 4, Scene 14). He hurries Eros to take his armor off, not put it on.

For she imagines Antony waiting for her, praising her courage, and laughing from the other side of death at the fickle "luck of Caesar." "Husband," she cries out, "I come," claiming for the first and last time in the play the sanction of that title for their guilty love. She is entitled to use it, she says, because she is willing to die for it.

> Comment

"I am fire and air," she describes herself, "my other elements/ I give to baser life." This description of her singleminded resolve to die completes another pattern of **imagery**. She refers to the once popular physiology which thought of man as composed of four basic elements and their combinations, which produced the "humors." The four elements were air, fire, earth and water. The first two were light, hot, and dry; the latter were heavy, cold, and wet. Antony, in his first appearance (Act 1, Scene 1, Lines 35-36), swore his love for Cleopatra by contrasting "dungy earth" and its kingdoms with the nobility of his passion And at the beginning of this scene (Line 7), Cleopatra spoke of death as that which frees man from dependence on "the dung" of earth. Here the two come together. Her devotion and self-sacrifice have purified her love for Antony of any dross or baseness. And so her death will free her spirit from any dependence on her body.

She gathers her faithful serving-women into a last farewell embrace. The moment is too charged with emotion for poor, fragile Iras: She dies on the spot of a broken heart. Almost playfully Cleopatra chides her; if she is the first to meet Antony beyond the grave, he will bestow on her "that kiss/ Which is my heaven to have." She takes one of the deadly snakes from the basket and pulling open her robe, applies it to her breast.

Comment

There are no grounds for this in North or Plutarch. There she applies the asp to her arm. But there are ample dramatic grounds for Shakespeare's alteration. Its full dramatic force is felt in her hushing Charmian: "Peace, peace!/ Dost thou not see my baby at my breast,/ that sucks the nurse asleep?"

Impatient still at the asp's slow work, she takes another and applies it to her arm. But none is needed; in the middle of a question that expects no answer, she dies. "What should I stay ..." she begins, and Charmian finishes, "In this vile world?" Then the loyal maid closes her queen's eyes, straightens her royal crown, and applies an asp to her own arm. The guards come noisily in. When they see that "Caesar's beguiled," they call Dolabella. Just as he enters, Charmian dies. He precedes Caesar by only a moment. The conqueror and his train of followers march into a peaceful scene, not one of carnage. The queen, in full regalia, reclines on her couch, her maids dead at her feet, but nowhere a sign of blood. They seem asleep rather than dead. "She looks like sleep," the moved Caesar says, "As she would catch another Antony/ In her strong toil of grace." He wonders how death was caused; there are no usual signs of poisoning. Then Dolabella discovers the tell-tale swellings on her breast and arm, and a guard notices the trail of the asp on her skin and on the fig leaves in the basket. Caesar is resigned; "She shall be buried by her Antony." He is even moved by her death to some nobility of sentiment. "Their story is/ No less in pity than his glory which Brought them to be lamented."

Comment

Caesar is comparing the greatness of the compassion he feels for their tragic love with the glory of Antony, who brought its doom about.

And as his final act of the play, Caesar orders Dolabella to make arrangements for a state funeral and to observe "high order/ In this great solemnity."

SUMMARY

All the events in this scene should be seen in the light cast by Cleopatra's single-minded determination to die. Only in that way can we accurately judge her actions and motives. On the one side we have Cleopatra, who

1. determines to die;

2. deceives Proculeius that she wishes to live;

3. tries to kill herself with a dagger;

4. gains Dolabella's sympathy and confidence so as to discover Caesar's plans;

5. stages the scene with Seleucus so as to complete her deception of Caesar;

6. sends Charmian for the asps disguised as figs, as soon as Caesar is gone;

7. learns definitely that Caesar plans to take them alive to Rome;

8. bolsters up Iras's failing courage to die;

9. sends her maids for her royal costume while she brusquely gets rid of the clown;

10. bids goodbye to her ladies and dies.

Working against her determination to die we see Caesar's design to bring her back to Rome alive. It is executed:

1. by Proculeius, who is a trusted diplomat;

2. by Gallus and his soldiers who guard the tomb;

3. by Dolabella, who is sent to relieve Proculeius;

4. by Caesar himself, who does all he can to assure Cleopatra of his generosity and leniency.

This final scene also completes several patterns of **imagery** developed throughout the play:

1. the passage of life into death as day into night;

2. the contrast between the grossness of common life and the nobility of passionate love;

3. Cleopatra as Isis or moon-goddess, and the moon as an emblem of the waxing and waning of fortune;

4. the heroic size and grandeur of the protagonists.

ANTONY AND CLEOPATRA

CHARACTER ANALYSES

Mark Antony

The Antony we meet in this play is older than he was in *Julius Caesar*, hardened into middle age. He is still a great soldier, reputed the most successful general and statesman of his time: the "triple pillar of the world." But his reputation does not stop there. He is notorious also for his dissolute life, his sensuality and his vulgarity. We find him bedded in Alexandria, entangled in the charms of an infamous woman. He spends his nights in drinking and carousing and his days in feasting and making love. The business of state he neglects entirely. During the drinking bout in Pompey's galley we see more of this side of the man, when he conducts his Egyptian bacchanals. Meanwhile he leaves the soldiering to his lieutenants like Ventidius, but not without being jealous of their success. He is cruel and conscienceless in marrying the widowed sister of Caesar, Octavia, purely for political expediency, to gain a momentary advantage. He knows when he courts her that he will abandon her. For his reason and judgment, which brought him to the peak of fortune, have deserted him. After briefly struggling against his "dotage" on

Cleopatra, he succumbs utterly to her witchcraft. Her insistence on a sea battle at Actium; his lack of preparation against the less skillful but more alert generalship of Caesar; his desertion from battle to follow his frightened mistress; all demonstrate his infatuation and his folly. His streak of cruelty flashes out in his whipping of Tidias, and his gigantic rage engulfs Cleopatra at the end.

But that is not the whole man; not even the greater part of him; certainly not the most enduring. He has the great Roman virtue of stoicism. He accepts Fulvia's death quietly, but with sadness, shame, and regret. His own death he goes to lovingly, like a bridegroom to his bed. He can endure hardship without complaining, as Caesar knows. And Caesar learns as well that Antony can out - talk him and out - think him in argument. He is the more seasoned statesman of the two, and the abler diplomat. His reputation for soldiership among his foes - Pompey is chary of him - is not less than among his followers. Above all he is kind. Despite all his callous cynicism he is soft and generous. He treats Lepidus as an equal after Caesar has snubbed him; he releases his lieutenants from their loyalty after he has led them to defeat. More, he offers them gold and letters of introduction. His supreme act of generosity is his forgiveness of Enobarbus when his friend and comrade-in-arms deserts him for Caesar's side.

He is jealous of this good opinion among his troops and his friends; he guards his reputation even at death. His last words to his mistress show his concern to be remembered at the height of his career and not in decline. So his downfall is tied in with his loss of reputation. He brings it on himself, certainly, but we have the feeling that his doom comes from without. He falls from strength to weakness, from prosperity to disaster, from triumph to defeat, almost without struggling against it.

His judgment leaves him; his soldiers leave him; his closest friends leave him; this guardian spirit, Hercules, leaves him; and at the end he runs out of luck. Misfortune does not fall like a mountain to crush him or strike him from afar like lightning. Rather, the flood of success which has borne him high ebbs from under him and sinks him in the mire.

Cleopatra

The chief note in Cleopatra's character is her "infinite variety." She is quicksilver in her moods; she moves from teasing to jealous, to imperious, to sulking. She is mischievous and complacent, flagrant and subtle by turns. She chides loudly and flatters softly; she is wantonly carefree and deeply thoughtful. There is no trick she will not use, no deceit she boggles at. But there is a pattern in all of her variety: Or is it two patterns? Readers do not seem to agree. Does she exercise all of her charms and wiles to keep her lover or to deceive him? At first she urges him to hear the news from Rome, then she tries to prevent him from acting upon it. She cannot bear the thought of his leaving and tries desperately to keep him. Rather than rejoice at Fulvia's death - an obstacle to her desire removed - she is stunned and sees her own in Fulvia's misfortune. Antony is hardly gone when she is lovelorn, and has twenty messengers pursue him with tokens and remembrances. No one may speak slightingly of her absent lover without risking bloody teeth. She attacks the messenger who brings her news of Antony's marriage to Octavia, and in the depths of despair allows herself to be deluded about her rival. She insists on taking part in her lover's war, and when she has caused his defeat she pleads repentance for it. When Antony accuses her of flirting with Thidias, she protests her love and fidelity convincingly enough. Or is it that he wants to be convinced? She is genuinely afraid for her soldier before the first day's battle, and she greets him enthusiastically when he returns triumphant. We hear the infinite relief in her voice. And we hear it again in the midst of her grief at the end: grief that his downfall is complete, and relief that her death is certain.

Or is it? Does she sincerely intend, her lover dead, to follow him in death? She says so, but we wonder. We remember that Antony knew she was "cunning past man's thought." We remember that her former conquerors wound up her lovers. May she not, as Antony accuses her, conquer the conqueror Caesar on her bed? After Actium, when defeat looks certain, does she "pack cards" with Caesar? She flatters his ambassador Thidias, gives him her hand to kiss, promises Caesar her compliance. Would she have followed all the others to his camp, had not Antony caught her in the act? He believes so in his rage after the final defeat. He suspects her complicity in the mass surrender of his army without a show of resistance. Had she arranged this with Caesar? She tries to arrange other things with him: a meeting, her son's future, a false account of her wealth. Does she in those final hours in the tomb hope to make some deal with Caesar, not to spare her life, but to spare her feelings? She is afraid to return as Caesar's captive to Rome. That is the prospect that stands uppermost in her dread. She practices her arts on Dolabella to learn Caesar's confidential plans. When she is sure of his intentions, she resigns herself to death. Or perhaps she knew all along what her end would be; perhaps she baited Caesar for the sport, or to win some concessions for her son. After all, she had already prepared the asps, disguised so as to deceive the guards. And when she first sees Roman soldiers she draws a concealed dagger, to remove herself from their power.

Of course, there are no answers. Perhaps Shakespeare has left us with the questions because he did not know the answers himself, because Plutarch does not give any. Except for the final answer of all, which Cleopatra writes, obliterating her own mystery in the mystery of death, "as water is in water."

Enobarbus

Our first impression of this cynical soldier is all edge. A confessed woman-hater, he shows a steadier judgment of and a profounder insight into Cleopatra at first than does his lord. And he always understands Antony better than Antony understands himself. Frank, straightforward, not disillusioned because he never entertained any illusions, he is a man's man. He is not awed by rank or reputation; he never fears the truth-but one. He can move from scathing appraisal to rhapsodic praise when he describes Cleopatra's arrival in Tarsus. He sees from the beginning through Antony's marriage to Octavia. But he does turn the broad flank of his affection to the view once before he dies. Although he rages against Antony's blundering incompetence, he never ceases to love the man. Perhaps it is because he is so much like Antony; in his tragic end we foresee his master's. Both men have the solid military virtues. Yet working against these in both is a certain softness of sentiment or self-deception. This is the one truth he cannot face-about himself. Such men fall because, being the kind of men they are, they cannot reconcile the two sides of their characters. Enobarbus sees this conflict in Antony; he does not even suspect it in himself. A mercenary soldier, he has every reason to abandon a losing cause and back a winner while the betting is still open. Yet what can prudence argue against Antony's lovely gesture of friendship and forgiveness? What can self-interest claim against compassion? It is as if the soft center of the man were strangled in his iron shell.

Octavius

A man without a center, Octavius reacts to the surfaces of men and events. He is not deeply committed to anything but his own success. His only passion is ambition; besides his rival he is passionless. He has the great politician's virtues: patience, caution, industry, a hard head. He has a realistic respect for things as they are and enough opportunism not to flinch from using people. He sells his sister to Antony, quite frankly for political reasons. Nor does he care about Antony's love affairs, except as they affect the state. He deals "in lieutenantry," but he is astute in his choice of lieutenants. He lulls Pompey with a bogus peace treaty in order to defeat him when he is off his guard. He wants to use Cleopatra to magnify his own fame; for the woman herself he cares nothing. He is one man she cannot wrap around her finger. Those he cannot use he has only contempt for: One thinks of Lepidus, Enobarbus, the others who went over to his winning side. He is self-righteous because it comes easily to him. He sets about to revenge Octavia's insult as if he were the instrument of heavenly justice. In truth she has been the tool of his ambition. He will do nothing to excess. He remains aloof and sober at the party aboard Pompey's galley because carousing is beneath his dignity. He husbands himself. But he can suffer from overconfidence, as when he loses the first day's battle and when Cleopatra finally defeats him. But setbacks also are only superficial for this able man. His kind is not great, but destined to be successful.

Octavia

As Cleopatra's rival she is more important for what she is not than for what she is. Quite simply, she is not Cleopatra. Her "beauty, wisdom, modesty" are a foil to that queen's "infinite variety." She suffers quietly, bending all her weakness to the ends of helping her brother and remaining true to her husband. She speaks only some thirty lines in four scenes; she is the minor character in all of them. She is the victim: as much the victim of great policies as of Cleopatra's legendary power over men. So she must be got out of the way early. The structure of the play could not support a deeper, more sympathetic development of her personality. For she would become, in her injury, a rival to Cleopatra for the audience's affection if not admiration. And being a perfect example of Roman ethos, she might well tip the balance of sympathy away from Egypt and Antony.

Sextus Pompeius

The son of a great man, who reveals his own weakness in trying to claim his father's greatness. His weakness is not on the surface; he puts up a bluff and convincing show. But he lacks the fortitude to sustain it. He is as full of flourishes as of optimism. He foresees success for his conspiracy and even the news of Antony's return does not discourage him. He does not suspect - though Menas does, and his father would have - the treachery behind Caesar's peace treaty. There is a moral flourish in his rejection of Menas's plan to ambush the Triumvirs and murder them aboard his flagship. But it is as empty as the rest. He is not above wanting the profits of evil, but will not pay the price - for his honor's sake. He is the type of his rival, Caesar, the ambitious politician; but with a little too much surface and too little center, and without the essential ingredient: success.

Lepidus

Lepidus is a weakling; he is out of place among strong men. Pompey is betrayed by his weakness, but he makes a show of strength. Lepidus always shows his weakness. The perennial peacemaker, he risks offending no one. When Caesar criticizes Antony, he tries to defend the one without offending the other. Yet he loves neither. At their confrontation he is the essence of politeness, as if mere good manners could reconcile their differences. At the celebration of the peace treaty with Pompey he proves again that he has not the stuff of greatness; the others recognize it openly and make him the drunken butt of their jokes. He is no Caesar to recognize his limitations and respect them. He has an ostrich-like quality of ignoring unpleasantness in the hope it will disappear. And so he does; he disappears from the play, his absence hardly noticed, except in Caesar's sarcastic excuse for getting rid of him: that he had grown too cruel.

Minor Characters

Shakespeare keeps a number of minor characters moving in and out of the play to liven our interest. But he does not develop any of them too much, lest they distract our interest from the main characters. Each of these main characters is surrounded by friends, courtiers, attendants, messengers, advisers, whose incidental figures contribute something of their color and character to their master. Co-conspirators and henchmen of Pompey are the pirates Menecrates and Menas. The first is the more philosophical of the two, less the maker of events than their minister. His is the voice of prudence. Menas is the opposite extreme, a headlong Machiavellian schemer. He has the politician's caginess and opportunism. He pumps Enobarbus for information about the Triumvirate because he suspects the peace treaty is a trap; he sees the advantage he might take of the Triumvirs in their drunken carousing. And when his master can grasp neither, he abandons him. Caesar leans heavily on his advisers, perhaps because of his comparative youth and inexperience. Entering Lepidus's house to meet Antony, he says, "I do not know,/ Maecenas; ask Agrippa." And it is the more politic of the two, Agrippa, who puts forth the plan to marry Octavia to Antony. He defends his lord against Enobarbus's sarcasm when they eavesdrop on the Triumvirs' farewells. Both are rather provincial, for all their worldliness. They are astonished and a little scandalized by Enobarbus's account of Cleopatra's court. Maecenas may even display a little sentimental optimism in believing Octavia can hold Antony from Cleopatra. We watch the courtiers' characteristic weakness harden on them like fat when with Caesar's success their deference ripens into flattery. Thidias and Dolabella are accomplished ambassadors, diplomats chosen for their ability to attract and influence Cleopatra. Notice how Dolabella addresses the defeated queen as if she, not Octavia, were Antony's lawful wife: "Empress," he calls her. Antony's relationship to his followers is a friendlier one. He does not lean so heavily on their judgment-perhaps he should-as on their love. Ventidius is aware of this, and so sacrifices his better judgment to keep in his jealous master's good graces. Canidius withdraws his loyalty when he finds Antony's judgment lost. Scarus' immediate wrath over Actium spends itself and though his better judgment tells him to desert, his love keeps him by his lord. But the image of love and loyalty is Eros-Eros who independently fetches Cleopatra to comfort Antony after Actium; Eros who spends his last hours weeping over Antony's disgrace. And it is Eros whose last act of love overcomes his judgment when he kills himself rather than kill his friend. Cleopatra's court is all women except for Mardian, who is all but a woman, and Alexas, who is "much unlike" Mark Antony. One epicene man in a hive of women, just as Octavia is one colorless woman in an army of men. And then Alexas deserts to Caesar, leaving only Charmian and Iras. Charmian is the more robust of the two, the outspoken "wild bedfellow." She keeps her head when Iras is near hysteria. As the soothsayer predicts, she outlives her mistress, but only by a minute. Iras is the quieter, more fragile girl. She panics easily; she has to be reassured constantly; her courage is always on the point of breaking. Yet she knows what is finally expected of her, and precipitate as always, she does not wait for the asp. The very expectation of death, grief in anticipation, kills her. The soothsayer and clown are not characters at all, in the sense of developed personalities. They are stage **conventions** which Shakespeare uses to create mood and atmosphere. Around the wizard hovers the odor of incense, some mystery of the East. As usual in tragedy, he enigmatically sees the end of the play in its beginning. The clown is a low comedian, probably much beloved by the audience. He takes some of the tension out of Cleopatra's death scene, and by contrast he adds some. He gives the audience something to laugh at legitimately, yet when he takes his gallows humor with him, he leaves the stage darker than before.

ANTONY AND CLEOPATRA

CRITICAL COMMENTARY

Antony and Cleopatra has had an oddly uneven history. It has meant many different things to different men through the years and produced a broad spectrum of values and interpretations. These readings can be grouped pretty generally into three categories; of course, these categories will often overlap. In rough chronological order the three points of view from which critics have viewed the play are: (1) the moral; (2) the esthetic; (3) the political.

DRYDEN

The first great commentator on Shakespeare's play was the seventeenth century playwright and man of letters, John Dryden. He expressed his dissatisfaction with *Antony and Cleopatra* by writing a play of his own on the same story, mending what he thought were the flaws in Shakespeare's version. The title he gave his play shows immediately how he construed its **theme**: All For Love. And its subtitle is a commentary on what Antony has lost in order to pursue his tragic love for Cleopatra: or, The World Well Lost. He recasts the materials of Shakespeare's play so as to make sharper the clash between the Egyptian queen and the Roman Empire, between love and honor; and to make more dramatic Antony's tragic choice. Dryden and his time were chiefly concerned, as he says in his Preface, with "the excellency of the moral: For the chief persons represented were famous patterns of unlawful love; and their end accordingly was unfortunate." Dryden retells the tale so as to make clearer that Antony and Cleopatra are punished at the end for their crimes: "The crimes of love, which they both committed, were not occasioned by any necessity, or fatal ignorance, but were wholly voluntary; since our passions are, or ought to be, within our power." This moral interpretation of the play as the downfall or punishment of its guilty **protagonists** and the triumph of the Roman ideal of honor became a model for later critics.

Dryden was also dissatisfied with the form of Shakespeare's play. He felt its rambling looseness of construction not only obscured the moral **theme** but violated the rules of dramatic composition. These rules were known as the unities of action, place and time, and required that the story dramatized in a tragedy should be single and simple with no subplots, and that it all occur in the same place during a single day, or circuit of the sun. So Dryden made his play conform to these rules of dramatic composition because, for moral reasons, he conceived of it as a tragedy. About All for Love, he says, "The fabric of the play is regular enough ... and the unities of time, place and action more exactly observed" than in Shakespeare's version.

Dryden's play was a great success and so conformed to the tastes and **conventions** of his time and later that it took the place of *Antony and Cleopatra* on the London stage until 1759. Since 1606/7 when it was first performed, there is no record of a major performance of Shakespeare's play until it was revived by David Garrick in 1759. It was promptly dropped again. Despite a lavish and expensive production and five months of preparation, the play "did not seem to give ye Audience any great pleasure or draw any applause." But it is clear that the interpretation of the play had changed. It was no longer the solemn moral tragedy as conceived by Dryden but a spectacular theatrical showpiece.

JOHNSON

This change is clearer in the brief notes of Samuel Johnson, inserted in his 1765 edition of the play. He believed that the play's "power of delighting is derived from the frequent changes of the scene ..." The reason he stresses the spectacle - the hurry of the action and variety of incident - is that he conceives of the play not as a tragedy but as a history, or chronicle play. "The events, of which the principal are described according to history, are produced without any art of connection or care of disposition." So Shakespeare, he feels, was retelling the history of the period, not the tragic defeat of its title characters. Consequently, for him these characters diminish in importance: "No character is very strongly discriminated," he says. But though the conception of what Shakespeare was doing has changed, the old moral interpretation shows itself still in Johnson's comments when he speaks of "the feminine arts, some of which are too low, which distinguish Cleopatra ..."

COLERIDGE

S. T. Coleridge continues this tradition in the early part of the nineteenth century, but in his *Notes on Shakespeare* the moral judgment is mellower and the opposition between chronicle and tragedy is less extreme. Cleopatra is still the model of unlawful passion, but now the passion is more pardonable. "The sense of criminality in her passion is lessened by our insight into its depth and energy, at the very moment that we cannot but perceive that the passion itself springs out of the habitual craving of a licentious nature ..." Her love for Antony is guilty also in that it is not a natural or spontaneous emotion but one nurtured and supported by her own wiles and associations. Although he condemns their love as an unlawful one, Coleridge does not read their suffering and death as an ignominious punishment for it. But he does group the play with the great tragedies, and says that in "its strength and vigor of maturity" it rivals Macbeth, Lear, Hamlet, and Othello. It is this strength and vigor of the play's style which expresses the depth and energy of the hero's unlawful passion and which makes it pardonable, though still unlawful. Coleridge is the first to feel that the magnificent poetry of the play, its style, makes the immoral characters magnificent in their doom. He says of this style: Feliciter Audax, or "daring but successful." The style is daring because it tries to meld together two distinct forms: tragedy and history. It is successful because Shakespeare's close allegiance to his historical source does not weaken its dramatic structure. It is both history and tragedy at once. By means of its daring style, history comes alive: "numerous momentary flashes of nature" counteract "the historic abstraction." And to show that it demonstrates surpassing judgment as well as genius, Coleridge compares it to Dryden's more regular play.

HAZLITT

William Hazlitt, a contemporary of Coleridge, shares his admiration for the poetry of *Antony and Cleopatra*. "This is a very noble play," he says of it, but does not rank it in the first class of Shakespeare's plays as Coleridge does. Hazlitt points out particularly how well the leading characters are realized: they "breathe, move and live." And Cleopatra is the masterpiece among them. Her "whole character is the triumph of the voluptuous, of the love of pleasure and the power of giving it, over every other consideration." He describes the variety with which Shakespeare has endowed her. "She is voluptuous, ostentatious, conscious, boastful of her charms, haughty, tyrannical, fickle. The luxurious pomp and gorgeous extravagance of the Egyptian queen are displayed in all their force and luster, as well as the irregular grandeur of the should of Mark Antony." We sense here the note of moral censure rising in the burden of his praise. The note grows louder when he says, "Antony's headstrong presumption and infatuated determination to yield to Cleopatra's wishes to fight by sea instead of land, meet a merited punishment ..." But whatever their vices, the virtues of the poetic style gloss them over. We admire these weak or flawed characters because of the poetry they speak. It is this poetic conception of character which is able "partly perhaps to place the effeminate character of Mark Antony in a more favorable light ..." Like Antony, Cleopatra "had great and unpardonable faults, but the grandeur of her death almost redeems them. She learns from the depth of despair the strength of her affection." But only "almost."

Hazlitt does not read the play as a strict tragedy because it conforms to known facts. He calls it rather Shakespeare's finest historical play: "He made poetry the organ of history." But the history is so reshaped by the poetry as to bring out its latent significances. And so, simple chronicle becomes a contest between Roman pride and Eastern magnificence. This **epic** quality of its dimensions, he judges, derives from its disregard of the dramatic unities of time and place.

LATER CRITICISM

The late nineteenth century critic A. C. Bradley echoes much of what Coleridge and Hazlitt have observed. He speaks of "the immense scale and world-wide issue of the conflict," i.e., its **epic** proportions. This epic quality makes itself felt in other ways: in the absence of dramatic action or dramatization of historical fact in Acts 1 to 3; in the defectively loose construction of Acts 3 and 4. The outward conflict of the play is the political struggle for power; we turn for relief from it to the real center of the drama, the fate of the lovers who are sure to lose it. The contrast between these two dramas, venal politics and tragic love, has two results: first, it blunts our feeling of the greatness of Antony's fall from prosperity; second, it emphasizes the positive element in the final tragic impression, the element of reconciliation.

But Bradley does not group this play with Shakespeare's four great tragedies, because it fails to produce the overwhelming tragic effect. The moral judgment of the play is too much softened by an admiration and sympathy for the lovers for us to condemn their love entirely; yet that live is too destructive for us to applaud it. We cannot rejoice to see them destroyed; but we know it must be so. "It is plain that the love of Antony and Cleopatra is destructive; that in some way it clashes with the nature of things; that while they are sitting in their paradise like gods, its walls move inward and crush them at last to death. This is no invention of the moralizing critics ... But then to forget because of it the other side, to deny the name of love to this ruinous passion, to speak as though the lovers had utterly missed the good life, is to mutilate the tragedy and to ignore a great part of its effect upon us. For we sympathize with them in their passion." But our pity ought not blind our moral judgment. "With all our admiration and sympathy for the lovers, we do not wish them to gain the world. It is better for the world's sake, and not less for their own, that they should fail and die." The softening or romanticizing of the moral judgment has gone quite far since Dryden rewrote the play as a conflict of unlawful love and honor. And along with this change in the play's meaning has gone a revision of the moral caliber of the characters, especially Cleopatra. She has been transformed by this critical trend from a whore-a pattern of unlawful love-to a constant and noble lover. Bradley believes that in Act 5 "she becomes unquestionably a tragic character, but, it appear to me, not till then." And he finds "what raises Cleopatra at last into pure tragedy is, in part, that which some critics have denied her, her love for Antony."

TWENTIETH CENTURY CRITICISM

Thus by the start of the twentieth century the critical lines are drawn. There are two general interpretations of the play which correspond to the two views, Egyptian and Roman, expressed in the play. The moralist school adopts the Roman view that Antony's love is mere dotage, infatuation, his downfall the ignoble effect of debauchery. They stress his growing folly and his cruelty. Cleopatra becomes simply a harlot to their eyes; a very successful, even a great, one, but still a harlot. Her death, like his, is a just and inevitable end. Their method is historical. Because of the growing romanticism, this school goes back to Shakespeare's own times for evidence to establish its case. The aesthetic school develops the Egyptian point of view. These critics acknowledge much of the moral censure of their colleagues, but try to show that the usually severe condemnation of such love and of the lovers' actions generally, are softened and even overcome by the magnificent poetry which they speak. The final scenes of the play, they maintain, are a hymn of praise to the nobility of love's sacrifice. Though the lovers die, no moral censure is possible. In fact we sympathize with them completely at the end. A third school of critics, using the same historical method as the moralists, tries to escape the dilemma by interpreting the play from neither the moral nor the aesthetic but the political point of view. They are closer in their conclusions to the former group than to the latter.

THE MORALIST SCHOOLS

The greatest of those to speak against anachronistic criticism and to emphasize the theatrical virtues of the play as originally staged is Harley Granville-Barker. His Preface is still a classic piece of theatrical direction and criticism. He feels that "a larger **theme** than the love-story is being worked out" in the spacious field of world politics. Their balance has been lost, he says, by arbitrary division of the play's continuous action into acts and scenes. These two **themes** are abreast - "Antony's concord with Caesar seen in the wane while, Cleopatra, spiderlike, sits spinning a new web for him ..." However Barker's preoccupation with theatrical effects leads him away from an interpretation which depends upon poetic effects derived from a close study of the **imagery**. Antony dies as he has lived, "a soldier and a sportsman - and a gentleman by his lights - to the end." He greets his death stoically: Shakespeare spares him no ignominy; yet out of it rises ... a man set free of debt to fate ..." Barker does not try to resolve the contradictions or inconsistencies in Cleopatra's character by making her either harlot or saint. The effort of the actress must be rather to maintain the antitheses in her disposition and her infinite variety. "From wantonness, trickery and folly, Shakespeare means to lift her to a noble end. But, even in doing it, he shirks no jot of the truth about her." And her final resignation, even joyful acceptance of death, is the "failure's contempt for success." Her death is not "high spiritual tragedy." She dies "defiant, noble in her kind, shaming convenient righteousness, a miracle of nature that - here is the tragedy - will not be reconciled to any gospel but its own."

E. K. CHAMBERS

Another of the moralist critics is E. K. Chambers, who did so much in the history of the Elizabethan theatre. Of Antony he says, "the instinct of domination and the instinct of sex are at odds in him; and if he chooses the worser course it is not without clear consciousness on his part of the issues at stake." Of Cleopatra, that she "is so conceived that she is fit to mate with her lover" because "love that is to be the scourge of the world, even if it is rooted in sensuality, must possess the attributes of majesty." "She is half courtesan and half a grande amoureuse." Their hypnotic love is "baleful" but so intense as to make it "worthy" of the tragedy. Of the play itself he concludes that in it, "Honor of chivalry and love of women ... must stand their arraignment ... Shakespeare returns to the double **theme** to strip the mask of worship from the specter of egoism, and to indict passion as the ruin of greatness ..."

OTHER CRITICS

More recent rebels against canonization of *Antony and Cleopatra* are John F. Danby, L. C. Knights, Franklin M. Dickey and Willard Farnham. Danby sees in the play opposites juxtaposed, mingled and married: "Then from the very union which seems to promise strength, dissolution flows." This polarity of opposites he calls "the World," represented by Caesar and Rome, and "the Flesh," represented by Cleopatra and Egypt. Antony must choose between them; but because neither would exhaust his potential, either would prove his downfall. So Shakespeare, he concludes, is not censuring either, but both, the very choice that limits itself. Antony and Cleopatra are both strumpet and fool and love's champions; or rather the play as a whole is Shakespeare's statement that such judgment may not be made.

L. C. Knights applauds Danby's conclusion, blames the romantic fallacy on the misinterpretation of Cleopatra's final speech as the total meaning of the play rather than merely one part of it. Antony's passion he describes as self-centered, self-consuming, especially after the battle of Actium: "At the superb close, Cleopatra-both empress and lass unparalleled-is an incarnation of sexual passion, of those primeval energies that are both necessary and destructive, that insistently demand fulfillment in their own terms, and, by insisting on their own terms, thwart the fulfillment that they seek."

Dickey's researches into cultural and literary history lead him to conclude, on the bases of classical and medieval authorities, and Elizabethan moral philosophy, that "Cleopatra appears again and again as wanton and a sorceress, who employed all the conscious arts of love to keep Antony ensnared." The Elizabethan spectator, he claims, "instead of seeing *Antony and Cleopatra* as patterns of nobility and of deathless love ... must have seen them as patterns of lust, of cruelty, of prodigality, of drunkenness, of vanity, and, in the end, of despair."

Willard Farnham's comments directly oppose him to Bradley. He finds the play not a drama of their love but of Antony's rise and fall in the struggle for world power after he meets Cleopatra. Shakespeare "does not show the world to be, to the losers, as nothing compared to their love." That love, "like themselves, never ceases to be deeply flawed, however much it becomes capable of arousing admiration." He rejects the romantic or

"Egyptian" view because "it was not the tendency of the age in which Shakespeare wrote to wash out the faults of Antony and Cleopatra in romantic sentiment ... Nor can it be said with truth that the final effect of Shakespeare's play is a romantic washing out of the faults of his hero and heroine." His sympathy for them does not save them from his moral judgment. Their downfall and suffering in this last of the tragedies are not the instruments of a mysterious and capricious destiny but the inexorable working out of a flaw in character.

AESTHETIC SCHOOL

The aesthetic school of interpretation, which corresponds to the Egyptian point of view, is anticipated by an early historical critic whose study of the relation between the play and its sources is still standard. M. W. MacCallum rejects the moralist view of alternatives: "If [their] love were not mutual, Antony would be merely the toy of the courtesan, Cleopatra merely the toy of the sensualist. But in point of fact, it is mutual and sincere." And like the later romanticizers, he feels that in the final scenes, "their oneness of heart and feeling is indeed ... complete, and their love is transfigured" by the beauty and nobility of the poetry.

The aesthetic school really flourished in the 1930s with an increased interest in Shakespeare's plays as poetry rather than theatre. Caroline Spurgeon reads the play primarily for its **imagery** and discovers a number of thematic images which establish the background or atmosphere of the play. Chief among these is "the world," mentioned forty-two times, and always giving the impression of "the expanse of the world and the tremendous consciousness of power on the part of the characters." The "imperial **theme**" is established by references to the grandeur of empire. Mark Van Doren later elaborated on both these **themes** in his interpretation of the play. Another image which provides tone for the play is "the Herculean hero," the giantlike dimensions of *Antony and Cleopatra*, which also provides Eugene M. Waith with the material for his study. W. H. Clemen, a German critic, expands the method and conclusions of Spurgeon. Besides creating atmosphere, the **imagery** "is symbolically related to the characters, serves their self-interpretations and the expression of their feelings." He is not troubled by the ambiguity of Cleopatra's character. "She is neither solely queen, nor solely harlot, nor solely witch, but unites in her person all these contrasting natures."

G. K. KNIGHT

An extreme example of the aesthetic school is G. W. Knight. A close student of the **imagery** of the play, he draws from it large philosophical conclusions as to Shakespeare's meaning. He finds in Cleopatra a metaphysical, not moral, good-a good of totality. She is good in the same large way one might say life is good, or the universe is good, not because it contains no suffering or bad times, but because from retrospect even these experiences are worth having. Cleopatra is a personification blent of good and evil; her "perfection flowers from totality, not exclusion." "Out of her varying moods, passions, experiences, one fact emerges: her serene love of Antony." The audience shares this transcendence of moral questions in the beauty of the poetry. "We watch as though from turrets of infinity, whence the ethical is found unreal and beauty alone survives." And of the characters he concludes, "In no play is the moral outlook so irrelevant as a means to distinguish the persons: it is rather an impossibility, has no meaning."

G. B. SHAW AND D. A. TRAVERSI

After Knight, much of the criticism of this school seems bent on proving G. B. Shaw's analysis of the play correct. In the Preface to his *Plays for Puritans*, Shaw says, with perhaps more than wind in his cheek, that "After giving a faithful picture of the soldier broken down by debauchery, and the typical wanton in whose arms such men perish, Shakespeare finally strains all his huge command of rhetoric and stage pathos to give a theatrical sublimity to the wretched end of the business, and to persuade foolish spectators that the world was well lost by the twain." D. A. Traversi would agree with much of this, with this proviso: that Shakespeare's "rhetoric" is poetry; his "pathos," tragic suffering; the "sublimity," real; the "strain," successful; the folly, wisdom. He certainly recognizes (as does Knight for that matter) the sordid **realism** of the play. "Antony's love is justified in terms of its intensity and vitality in spite of his continual awareness that Cleopatra is 'a whore of Egypt' ... in spite of the fact that his passion is the infatuation of a middle-aged soldier for a woman who had already served Julius Caesar's pleasure." Shakespeare, he admits, never disguises either Antony's incompetence or Cleopatra's corruption. But he believes both their venality and their stupidity are overcome by the brilliance of the poetry, the "poetic redemption," so to speak, of their love. Antony's "mad renunciation of practical affairs is balanced by the splendid assertion of his love," and Cleopatra's corruption becomes the fertile decay which breeds new life. So at the end "Antony's suicide becomes an integral part of the final lyrical assertion of the value and transcendence of passion. It looks forward to the poetry of Cleopatra's death ..." This welding of opposites in the play, incompetence with wisdom, promiscuity with love, sordid **realism** with the most exalted poetry, leads Traversi to conclude that *Antony and Cleopatra* is "the play in which Shakespeare came nearest to unifying his experience into a harmonious and related whole."

MAURICE CHARNEY

The latest and most extended statement of the aesthetic viewpoint is by Maurice Charney; it is also the soberest and most measured statement. He believes that neither Roman nor Egyptian viewpoint is wholly correct; the very positing of alternatives is wrong. "It is necessary," he says, "to hold both the Egyptian and Roman **themes** in the play together in the mind as a tragic unity. Either without the other makes for distortion and incompleteness. Taken alone, the Roman point of view simplifies the tragedy into a morality play, and the Egyptian one transforms the tragedy into a poem of transcendental love." It is impossible to hold one set of values as right and the other as wrong. "There is a quality of 'somber realism' here that is neither moralistic nor rhapsodic, and the tragic conflict is not conceived as an alternation between Love and Honor." And he concludes, "The tragic choices of this play are between different kinds of rightness."

Charney finds two distinct tragedies in the play. Antony's is largely political. And so with his death "rather than being resolved, the conflict between Egypt and Rome ceases to exist ... dissolved into an ecstatic poetic reality." This poetry of the lovers salvages their love and ennobles it. "Suicide is Cleopatra's tragic choice, and she is ennobled by it although she does not become a full-scale tragic **protagonist** as Antony does. Her tragedy is very clearly focused on this choice, whereas Antony is made to bear the burden of choice, responsibility, and guilt throughout the play. We may say, then, that Cleopatra begins as a temptress or enchantress rather than a tragic figure, but she is drawn up into tragedy by Antony's death." Whereas Farnham saw this as the last of Shakespeare's great tragedies, Charney sees it in certain respects as the first of his late romances.

THE POLITICAL VIEW

Avoiding these two alternatives, the moralist and the aesthetic, the political viewpoint gives greater weight to the world-power struggle in the play; Antony's downfall becomes political or military, Cleopatra just one more of his conquests. Lord David Cecil, seeing the play as more panorama than drama, tries to explain its meaning in this way. He believes that the great variety of mood, the vast distances covered, the swiftly changing scenes, the absence of unity, pattern, or dramatic significance, stem from Shakespeare's historical attitude to his subject. He is retelling history, not creating drama. However, the play does achieve a unity and a significance of sorts, and this he believes is due to Shakespeare's single presiding **theme**. "This theme is not love; it is success." The real conflict of the play is "the chaotic spectacle of the great world convulsed in the struggle for power and happiness ..." And so he concludes, "The real test is between Antony and Octavius." Of the lovers, he says, "Antony's love is a self-indulgent passion that weakens his will and blinds his judgment. While Cleopatra is, by a strict moral standard, a vain, worthless, capricious coquette ..." Yet they are transformed, he feels, by Shakespeare's mature poetic style. Shakespeare's "conclusion seems to be that it is impossible to be certain in our judgment of Antony's conduct." Thus he avoids either the moralist or the aesthetic point of view.

Another political critic is T. J. B. Spencer. He buttresses his position with historical scholarship. In Shakespeare's time, he tells us, "ancient, in particular, Roman history was used as the material for political lessons, because it was one of the few bodies of consistent and continuous historical material available." Because the audience was well acquainted and concerned with it, "When Shakespeare turned ... to Roman history as the subject of plays, he was touching upon grave and provocative problems of political morality, already much discussed." So much for the audience; the play also reveals a political bias. Shakespeare's concentration on the two title characters "does not impair our impression of the imperial **theme**. Cleopatra... does not dominate the play. Her self-centered nature is even more apparent because the real subject of the play is conflict in Antony, who is repeatedly confronted with a choice between his love for Cleopatra and his loyalty to the political and moral dignity of Rome." Here the political comes rather close to the moral; Spencer also shares some of the attitudes of the aesthetic school. "The poetry of the play exalts love. The splendor of language given to Cleopatra and to Antony, captures our imaginative sympathy for the losing side, for the 'wrong side'." But despite the poetry it remains the 'wrong' side, because it lost.

ANTONY AND CLEOPATRA

ESSAY QUESTIONS AND ANSWERS

Question: Why and how does Shakespeare make the loser, rather than the winner, the hero of the play?

Answer: If we judge the hero to be the character who wins in the end, then Caesar would seem to be the hero. But is success necessarily the sign of the hero, the stamp of the author's approval? It may be that the virtues and dispositions which a man requires to become successful may not be those which the author thinks are the best or most important in the play. Caesar has all of those qualities which fit him for success. He is sober, cautious, temperate, prudent; he has no excesses. We can foresee in the scene on Pompey's flagship that these virtues will win out in the end. Even luck is with him, as the soothsayer tells Mark Antony. When the two are competing, Caesar's guardian spirit always bests Antony's. Caesar is industrious and persevering. And while these qualities tend to make him aloof from other people, a little pompous and self-righteous, no one can deny they are admirable traits, as the world goes, and that he is an able man. On the other hand, Mark Antony is all excess. He drinks, feasts, wantons, and carouses too much; he neglects all his responsibilities and lets important state business slide. He alienates his friends, jeopardizes his soldiers, breaks Octavia's heart. He sacrifices everything he has become for the doubtful love of one woman. This is not admirable nor exemplary as the world goes. Yet Antony, even in his downfall, triumphs over Caesar. For in his very excess, his largeness of appetite and his largeness of soul, he demonstrates a far greater capacity for love, for suffering, for self-sacrifice. Neither Antony nor the audience envies Caesar his victory at the end: "I hear him mock/ The luck of Caesar," Cleopatra says. Shakespeare has shown through his tragic hero that true greatness is beyond carping moral sanctions, that love triumphs over all, that suffering brings wisdom.

Question: Does Cleopatra love Antony or merely use him?

Answer: Shakespeare leaves some doubt about the relationship between Antony and Cleopatra. Plutarch says that Cleopatra first went to meet Antony intending to seduce him. She made him fall in love with her to avoid his wrath. Enobarbus implies this when he describes the meeting to Agrippa and Maecenas, and Cleopatra admits as much when, adorning herself for death, she says, "I am again for Cydnus, to meet Mark Antony." She boasts also of her conquests of former Roman conquerors, Julius Caesar and Pompey the Great. After her treachery at Actium, Antony accuses her of a triple infidelity: She left Julius Caesar for Pompey; she left Pompey when Antony conquered her; and now she will leave him for the next winner, Octavius Caesar. And he dies, forgiving her certainly, but perhaps still doubtful of her loyalty, unless Diomedes' brief "Which never shall be found" is enough to reassure him. For he takes for granted that she will seek her safety with Caesar. Shakespeare never says clearly whether she played a part in the mass surrender of Antony's troops in their final defeat. And her last hours in the monument are a patchwork of inconsistency. She says in Act 4, Scene 15, right after Antony's death, that she too is resolved to die by her own hand. But then we find her trying to make some arrangements with Caesar. It cannot be for her children, because in killing herself she abandons them to the "destruction" which Caesar threatens. It is never completely clear whether she commits suicide because she cannot live without Antony, or because she cannot live with Caesar. The reason may be that Shakespeare did not know himself, because the story he is dramatizing from Plutarch does not tell him. So rather than add anything untrue or change the original he incorporates the inconsistency into Cleopatra's character, where it enhances her cunning and her "infinite variety."

Question: How does Shakespeare contrast the two worlds of Egypt and Rome?

Answer: From the very first speech of the play in the mouth of the Roman soldier, Philo, Shakespeare is concerned to set off the world of Rome from the world of Egypt. In the course of the play these two places come to stand for two characteristic ways of life, two sets of values. He does this by contrasting the businesslike atmosphere of Rome, rife with political faction and intrigue, peopled by men of affairs, world-conquerors, with the indolent leisure of Egypt, where there is always time for sensual pleasures and lewd gossip, as in Act 1, Scene 2. Then again there are no women in the Roman scenes, except Octavia, and she is purposely made to seem modest and demure, a true example of Roman virtue. In Cleopatra's court, on the other hand, aside from the Romans, there is nothing but women and effeminate men. The eunuch, Mardian, and the effete Alexas are symbolic specimens of Egyptian manhood. Against the sober and rational atmosphere of Rome - the meeting between Antony and Caesar, between the Triumvirs and Pompey; is set the mystery and emotion of the East - the predictions of the soothsayer,

Cleopatra's treatment of the messenger. The Egyptian bacchanals in Pompey's galley and the fortune teller's advice to Antony are good examples of the contrast Shakespeare achieves. This contrast is achieved also between Octavia's utterly bare and unannounced arrival in Rome and the description of Cleopatra's arrival by barge at Tarsus on the River Cydnus. Besides, it is the prosaic Roman soldier who describes the gorgeous opulence and wasteful extravagance of the East. It is primarily here, in the **imagery**, that the contrast between Rome and Egypt takes place. Sexual allusions, descriptions of Nile's fertility and of its flora and fauna, lush images of wealth and ease, characterize Egypt as an earthly paradise. But there is in it an element of sordid **realism**, the corruption and decay-Nile's "ooze and slime" - out of which this fertile paradise is generated. Rome is characterized by martial **imagery** and political rhetoric. We hear it in the machinations of the Pompeian conspiracy, in the confrontation between Antony and Caesar, in the signing of the peace treaty, in the subsequent political infighting. We see it in the sober qualities of the Roman soldiers and politicians. The final scene in the monument depicts the contrast in small: the gorgeous dress of Cleopatra, the exotic method of her suicide, are juxtaposed to the coarse soldiers who discover her. And the note of triumph is in Charmian's voice when she dies exclaiming, "Ah, soldier!"

Question: Account for the loose construction of the play, especially the middle acts.

Answer: The unusually large number of scenes in Acts 2, 3 and 4 and their loose construction, criticized by A. C. Bradley as "defective," represent Shakespeare's solution to a dramatic problem posed by his material. As usual with him, he turns the obstacle to an advantage. His task is to dramatize the large and unwieldy body of prose narrative in North's translation of

Plutarch's *Life of Mark Antony*. He wants to be faithful to the broad scope of his source, its vast and complex political issues, and at the same time to shape this material into a dramatic story of Antony's tragic downfall. Since the story stretches across a long period of time and thousands of miles, Shakespeare shifts his scene from Alexandria to Rome, to Sicily, to Syria, to Athens, so as to follow the careers of his principal characters and to convey some sense of the scope of his action. Besides being numerous, the scenes are fragmentary. Mark Van Doren shows how this fragmentation extends even into the rhythms of the poetry, as if the canvas were so large it could only be seen in snatches. Shakespeare could move so freely because of the absence of scenery and other theatrical effects on his stage. He could rely on the imagination of his audience and the descriptive power of his poetry to create the sense of locale he desired. So these scenes-Egypt versus Rome-become symbolic of the conflicting values of the play. And the vast scale of the action reinforces the imperial **theme**, the grandeur of the lovers, and the image of Antony as a demigod, the Herculean hero. Thus Shakespeare remains true to his source, yet economizes on it dramatically and makes its vast scope serve his dramatic purposes.

SUBJECT BIBLIOGRAPHY AND GUIDE TO RESEARCH PAPERS

Any research into *Antony and Cleopatra* should begin with an accurate and reliable edition of the play. A well-annotated text with especially helpful appendices (including relevant sections of North's translation of Plutarch's *Lives*) is the Arden Edition edited by M. R. Ridley (and R. H. Case) and published by *Harvard University Press*. The Pelican Shakespeare, a less expensive edition which is also very good, is published in paperback by Penguin Books and edited by Maynard Mack. Other worthwhile editions are the New Variorum, with an extensive apparatus, edited by Furness; and J. Dover Wilson's New Cambridge edition.

There are many books and articles of criticism on Shakespeare's Roman plays generally and on *Antony and Cleopatra* in particular. The following is a selection of the most important criticism, grouped according to subjects or research topics and arranged alphabetically by author.

SHAKESPEARE'S USE OF HIS SOURCES

Questions to consider: What were the sources for *Antony and Cleopatra*? How do we know which of them Shakespeare had read? How did he alter them to suit his own purposes?

Mac Callum, M. W. *Shakespeare's Roman Plays*. London, 1910.

Norman, A. M. Z. "The Tragedie of Cleopatra and the date of *Antony and Cleopatra*," *Modern Language Review*, LIV, 1959, 1-9.

Rees, J. "An Elizabethan eye-witness of *Antony and Cleopatra*?" *Shakespeare Survey*, VI, 1953, 91-3.

Schanzer, E. "Daniel's Revision of his Cleopatra," *Review of English Studies*, VII, 1957, 375-81.

Thomson, J. A. K. *Shakespeare and the Classics.* London, 1952.

RELIGIOUS AND ETHICAL BACKGROUND

Questions to consider: What is the ethical meaning of *Antony and Cleopatra*? What is Shakespeare's conception of Roman and Egyptian religious attitudes?

Couchman, G. W. "*Antony and Cleopatra* and the Subjective Convention," *Publications of the Modern Language Association*, LXXVI, 1961, 420-5.

Cunningham, D. G. "The Characterization of Shakespeare's Cleopatra," *Shakespeare Quarterly*, VI, 1955, 14.

Danby, John F. "The Shakespearean Dialectic. An Aspect of *Antony and Cleopatra*," *Scrutiny*, XVI, 1949, 196-213.

Dunno, E. S. "Cleopatra Again," *Shakespeare Quarterly*, VII, 1956, 227-233.

Knights, L. C. "On the Tragedy of *Antony and Cleopatra*," *Scrutiny*, XVI, 1949, 318-323.

Stempel, D. "The Transmigration of the Crocodile." *Shakespeare Quarterly*, VII, 1956, 59-72.

What is considered ethical, what unethical about the behavior of Cleopatra?

Granville-Barker, Harley. *Prefaces to Shakespeare.* Princeton, N. J., 1952, V. I.

Kirschbaum, Leo. "Shakespeare's Cleopatra," *Shakespeare Association Bulletin*, XIX, 1944, 161-71.

Lloyd, M. "Cleopatra as Isis," *Shakespeare Survey*, XII, 1959, 88-94.

Schucking, L. L. *Character Problems in Shakespeare's Plays.* London, 1922.

Stewart, J. I. M. *Character and Motive in Shakespeare.* London, New York, 1949.

Stoll, E. E. "Cleopatra," *Modern Language Review*, XXIII, 1928, 145-63. (Reprinted in *Poets and Playwrights.* Minneapolis, 1930.)

Does Shakespeare judge Antony's behavior moral or immoral?

Brown, Huntington. "Enter the Shakespearean Tragic Hero," *Essays in Criticism*, III, 1953 285-302.

Mac Lure, M. "Shakespeare and the Lonely Dragon," *University of Toronto Quarterly*, XXIV, 1955, 109-120.

Stein, A. "The Image of Antony: Lyric and Tragic Imagination," *Kenyon Review*, XII, 1959, 586-606.

Stirling, B. *Unity in Shakespearean Tragedy: the Interplay of* **Theme** *and Character.* N. Y., 1956.

Waith, Eugene M. *The Herculean Hero in Marlowe, Chapman, Shakespeare and Dryden*, N. Y., 1962.

THE POLITICAL BACKGROUNDS

Questions to consider: What are the politics of Antony? Of Octavius? How would the Elizabethan audience react to the power struggle between these two men? What is the author's judgment of their policies? How does Shakespeare's political judgment affect the moral meaning of the play?

Cecil, Lord David. *Antony and Cleopatra*. Glasgow, 1944. (Reprinted in *Poets and Storytellers*, N. Y., 1949.)

Charlton, H. B. *Shakespeare: Politics and Politicians*. English Association Pamphlet No. 72, Oxford UP, 1929.

Draper, J. W. "Political **Themes** in Shakespeare's Later Plays," *Journal of English and Germanic Philology*, XXV, 1936, 61-93.

Jorgensen, P. A. "Enobarbus' Broken Heart and the Estate of English Fugitives," *Philological Quarterly*, XXX, 1951, 387-392.

Phillips, J. E. *The State In Shakespeare's Greek and Roman Plays*. N. Y., 1940.

IMAGERY

Questions to consider: How does Shakespeare use figurative language to bring out the meaning of his play? How does auditory **imagery** contribute to this meaning? Why the vast distances involved? Why the sexual **imagery**? Why the martial **imagery**? What is the imperial **theme** of the play? How does the imagery add to the stature of the characters?

Bethell S. L. *Shakespeare and the Popular Dramatic Tradition*. Durham, N. C., 1944.

Charney, Maurice. *Shakespeare's Roman Plays*. Cambridge, 1961.

Jenkin, B. "*Antony and Cleopatra*: Some Suggestions on the Monument Scene," *Review of English Studies*, XXI, 1945, 1-14.

Knight, G. Wilson. *The Imperial **Theme***. London, 1951.

Leavis, F. R. "*Antony and Cleopatra*," *Scrutiny*, V, 1936-7, 158-69.

Lloyd, M. "The Roman Tongue," *Shakespeare Quarterly*, X, 1959, 461-8.

Spurgeon, Caroline. *Shakespeare's **Imagery***. Boston, 1958.

Traversi, D. A. *Approach to Shakespeare*. London, 1938.

Van Doren, Mark. *Shakespeare*. N. Y., 1939.

Walker, Roy. "The Northern Star: An Essay on the Roman Plays," *Shakespeare Quarterly*, II, 1951.

ADDITIONAL BIBLIOGRAPHY

Maxwell, J. C. "Shakespeare's Roman Plays: 1900-1956," *Shakespeare Survey*, X, 1957, 1-11.

Spencer, T. J. B. *The Roman Plays*. London, 1963.

ANTONY AND CLEOPATRA

GENERAL BIOGRAPHY AND CRITICISM

Alexander, P., *Shakespeare's Life and Art*, New York, 1961. Development of Shakespeare from apprentice to mature artist.

Brooks, C., "Shakespeare as a symbolist poet," *Yale Rev.*, June, 1945.

Chambers, E. K., *The Elizabethan Stage*, Oxford, 1923. A classic for the study of Shakespeare's stage problems.

Coleridge, S. T., *Shakespearean Criticism*, reprint, New York, 1961. An interesting study of the play from a nineteenth century critic's viewpoint.

Farnham, Willard, *Medieval Heritage of Elizabethan Tragedy*, New York, 1956. One of the most complete studies of the classical vs. medieval concept of tragedy. Excellent comments on *King Richard III*.

Goddard, Harold, *The Meaning of Shakespeare*, New York.

Green, V. H. H., *The Later Plantagenets*, London, 1955. Shows the weakness of the line that accounts for their fall from power.

Hazlitt, Wm., *Characters of Shakespeare's Plays*, modern reprint. Thinks *King Richard III* is better on the stage than read in quiet, as was then being urged by some.

Hughes, A. E., *Shakespeare and His Welsh Characters*. Interesting comments on the Duke of Richmond and his Welsh background.

Perry, Alice I., *Stage History of Shakespeare's King Richard The Third*, New York, 1909. This work gives a full account of the various acting editions of the play.

Rowse, A. L., *William Shakespeare*, New York, 1963. Gives an excellent re-evaluation of the critics' views on *King Richard III*.

Sprague, A. C., *Shakespearean Players and Performances*, Cambridge, 1954. An account of the late sixteenth century stage.

GENERAL: CLASSIC CRITICISM AND INTERPRETATION

Bradley, A. C. "Shakespeare's *Antony and Cleopatra*" in *Oxford Lectures on Poetry*. London, 1950.

Case, R. H. and M. R. Ridley. Introduction to the Arden edition of *Antony and Cleopatra*. Cambridge, Mass., 1955.

Chambers, E. K. *Shakespeare: A Survey*. London, 1925.

Charney, Maurice. *Shakespeare's Roman Plays*. Cambridge, Mass., 1961.

Coleridge, S. T. *Notes and Lectures upon Shakespeare*. London, 1849, V. I, 145-148.

Danby, John F. *Poets on Fortune's Hill*. London, 1952.

Dickey, Franklin M. *Not Wisely, But Too Well*. San Marino, Calif., 1957.

Dowden, Edward. *Shakespeare*. N. Y., 1881.

Dryden, John. Preface to *All for Love* in Mermaid Series. London, 1949-50

Farnham, Willard. *Shakespeare's Tragic Frontier*. Berkeley, Calif., 1950.

Granville-Barker, Harley. *Prefaces to Shakespeare*. Princeton, N. J., 1952, V. I.

Hazlitt, William. *Characters of Shakespeare's Plays*. London, 1957.

Holzknecht, Karl J. *The Background of Shakespeare's Plays*. N. Y., 1950.

Johnson, Samuel. *Samuel Johnson on Shakespeare* (ed. W. K. Wimsatt, Jr.). N. Y., 1960.

Knight, G. Wilson. *The Imperial* **Theme**. London, 1951.

Knights, Lionel C. *Some Shakespearean Themes*. Stanford, Calif., 1960.

Mac Callum, M. W. *Shakespeare's Roman Plays*. London, 1910.

Mack, Maynard. Introduction to the Pelican edition of *Antony and Cleopatra*. Baltimore, 1960.

Ribner, Irving. *Patterns in Shakespearean Tragedy*. N. Y., 1960.

Rosen, William. *Shakespeare and the Craft of Tragedy*. Cambridge, Mass., 1960.

Spencer, T. J. B. *Shakespeare: The Roman Plays*. London, 1963.

Spurgeon, Caroline. *Shakespeare's* **Imagery**. Boston, 1958.

Symons, Arthur. "*Antony and Cleopatra*," in *Studies in the Elizabethan Drama*. London, 1920.

Traversi, D. A. *Approach to Shakespeare*. London, 1938.

Van Doren, Mark. *Shakespeare*, N. Y., 1939.

Wilson, Harold S. *On the Design of Shakespearean Tragedy*. Toronto, 1957.

Readings In Critical Methods as Applied to Shakespeare

Auerbach, Erich, *Mimesis* (1953), Ch. 13, "The Weary Prince" (Prince Hal in *Henry IV, Part Two*).

Brooks, Cleanth, *The Well-Wrought Urn* (1947), Ch. 2, "The Naked Babe and the Cloak of Manliness," (a study of **imagery** in *Macbeth*).

Downer, Alan S., "The Life of Our Design: The Function of **Imagery** in the Poetic Drama," in *Shakespeare: Modern Essays in Criticism*, ed. Leonard Dean (1957).

Empson, William, *The Structure of Complex Words* (1951), chapters on "Fool in Lear," and "Honest in *Othello*."

Fergusson, Francis, *The Human Image in Dramatic Literature* (1957), Part II, "Shakespeare."

____*The Idea of a Theatre* (1949), Ch. 4, "'*Hamlet*, Prince of Denmark;' The Analogy of Action."

Granville-Barker, *Harley On Dramatic Method* (1956), Ch. 3, "Shakespeare's Progress."

Kitto, H. D. F., *Form and Meaning in Drama* (1956), Ch. 9 *"Hamlet."*

LIFE AND TIMES OF SHAKESPEARE

Chute, Marchette. *Shakespeare of London.* New York, 1956. A very interesting biography that also provides analysis of Shakespeare's world.

Halliday, F. E. *Shakespeare: A Pictorial Biography.* New York, 1956. Excellent pictures.

Fluchère, Henri. *Shakespeare and the Elizabethans.* New York, 1956. Relates Shakespeare to the other dramatists of his time and to the world in which they lived.

Spencer, Theodore. *Shakespeare and the Nature of Men.* New York, 1951. A discussion of the philosophical background of Shakespeare's England with particular emphasis on man's place in nature.

Trevelyan, G. M. *History of England, Volume II: The Tudors and the Stuart Era.* New York, 1953. A good account of the history of Tudor England.

Tillyard, E. M. *The Elizabethan World Picture.* New York, 1944. An excellent description of the concepts, attitudes, and manners in Shakespearean England, supplying important background material for the understanding of all Shakespeare's work.

SHAKESPEAREAN THEATER PRODUCTION

Adams, John Cranford. *The Globe Playhouse: Its Design and Equipment.* New York, 1942.

De Banke, Cecile. *Shakespearean Production, Then and Now. A Manual for the Scholar Player.* New York, 1953.

Hodges, C. Walter. *The Globe Restored.* New York, 1954.

Smith, Irwin. *Shakespeare's Globe Playhouse. A Modern Reconstruction in Text and Scale Drawings.* New York, 1956.

These books describe the ways in which Shakespeare's plays were originally produced, and De Banke's account includes helpful suggestions for the modern producer.

SHAKESPEARE'S HISTORY PLAYS

Campbell, Lily B. *Shakespeare's Histories: Mirrors of Elizabethan Policy.* San Marino, California, 1947. An excellent description of the development of historiography in the English Renaissance, with a separate chapter on Henry V analyzed as the ideal victorious king.

Chambers, E. K. *Shakespeare: A Survey.* New York, 1959. A collection of essays on various Shakespeare plays, including an excellent chapter on Henry V in relation to patriotism in sixteenth century England.

Holzknecht, Karl J. *The Backgrounds of Shakespeare's Plays.* New York, 1950. A particularly useful account of the role of chroniclers and writers of popular history works for the theater in Tudor England. Shakespeare is seen in perspective with other men also concerned with historical themes.

Schelling, R. E. *The English Chronicle Play.* New York, 1902. An interesting discussion of the **genre** of the chronicle play flourishing before and during Shakespeare's lifetime.

Tillyard, E. M. W. *Shakespeare's History Plays*. London, 1956. An analysis of the myth of the Tudor Monarchy and the men who celebrated it in chronicle and drama, including Shakespeare. There is an excellent chapter on *Henry V* in this connection.

Traversi, Derek. *From Richard II to Henry V Stanford*, California, 1957. An exploration of the dominant **themes** in Shakespeare's **epic** of English history, with an interesting chapter emphasizing the moral development of the character of Henry V.

www.ingramcontent.com/pod-product-compliance
Lightning Source LLC
LaVergne TN
LVHW021715060526
838200LV00050B/2673